CRAFTING A
Dream Wedding

quick & easy projects and creative ideas

Susan Cousineau

NORTH LIGHT BOOKS
CINCINNATI, OHIO
www.artistsnetwork.com

About the Author

Susan Cousineau *is a freelance designer and author who lives with her husband, Tom, and their very spoiled pets in the picturesque town of Fort Frances, Ontario.*

CRAFTING A DREAM WEDDING is Susan's fourth title with North Light Books. Her previous books include EASY CHRISTMAS CRAFTS, SPOOKY HALLOWEEN CRAFTS and ENCHANTED GARDEN CRAFTS, along with numerous other instructional craft booklets she has authored with various publishers over the years. In addition, Susan is a regular contributor to several national craft magazines. Her educational credits include an honors degree in business administration and a diploma in computer graphic design.

Susan hopes this book will inspire you to create the beautiful wedding of your dreams.

 Published by North Light Books, an imprint of F+W Publications, Inc., 4700 East Galbraith Road, Cincinnati, Ohio 45236. (800) 289-0963. First edition.

09 08 07 06 05 5 4 3 2 1

Library of Congress Cataloging-in-Publication Data

Cousineau, Susan.
Crafting a dream wedding / by Susan Cousineau.-- 1st ed.
p. cm.
Includes index.
ISBN 1-58180-644-2
1. Handicraft. 2. Wedding decorations. I. Title.
TT149.C59 2005
745.594'1--dc22
2005000951

Distributed in Canada by Fraser Direct
100 Armstrong Avenue
Georgetown, ON, Canada L7G 5S4
Tel: (905) 877-4411

Distributed in the U.K. and Europe by David & Charles
Brunel House, Newton Abbot, Devon, TQ12 4PU, England
Tel: (+44) 1626 323200, Fax: (+44) 1626 323319
Email: mail@davidandcharles.co.uk

Distributed in Australia by Capricorn Link
P.O. Box 704, S. Windsor, NSW 2756 Australia
Tel: (02) 4577-3555

Editor: Jessica Gordon
Cover Designer: Leigh Ann Lentz
Interior Designer: Mary Barnes Clark
with assistance from Leigh Ann Lentz
Production Coordinator: Robin Richie
Photographers: Christine Polomsky, Tim Grondin, Greg Grosse & Hal Barkan
Stylist: Nora Martini

metric conversion chart

to convert	to	multiply by
Inches	Centimeters	2.54
Centimeters	Inches	0.4
Feet	Centimeters	30.5
Centimeters	Feet	0.03
Yards	Meters	0.9
Meters	Yards	1.1
Sq. Inches	Sq. Centimeters	6.45
Sq. Centimeters	Sq. Inches	0.16
Sq. Feet	Sq. Meters	0.09
Sq. Meters	Sq. Feet	10.8
Sq. Yards	Sq. Meters	0.8
Sq. Meters	Sq. Yards	1.2
Pounds	Kilograms	0.45
Kilograms	Pounds	2.2
Ounces	Grams	28.3
Grams	Ounces	0.035

A Wedding Story

As I begin to write this manuscript, I can't help but smile as I think back to the memory of my grandmother as she shared her wedding day story with me. Her small, no-frills wedding ceremony seemed far less important than those potatoes that had to be planted the very next day. And a honeymoon... who ever heard of such a silly thing back then?

As my husband Tom and I celebrate our twentieth anniversary (yes, I was a VERY young bride!), my thoughts turn back to our own wedding day. So much has changed since then. Lavishly embellished princess-style dresses were all the rage in wedding apparel, in contrast to the sleek, sophisticated gowns so popular today.

Our large church wedding, although very lovely, was quite a formal and traditional affair, a far cry from the casual, free-spirited ceremonies many couples choose today. Back then, I had never even heard of the term "destination wedding," let alone envisioned a wedding ceremony on a roller coaster, in a hot-air balloon, or under the sea! Yet that's what makes planning a wedding today so exciting—the fact that anything goes!

Now that you're planning to tie the knot, it's time to decide how your wedding day story will unfold. Regardless of whether you choose a large, formal affair rich in tradition or a smaller, more casual celebration, remember to let your own unique personality and style shine through every step of the way.

Happy Wedding Day!

Acknowledgments

I would like to express my heartfelt thanks to all of the talented folks at North Light Books who made this book possible: Tricia Waddell for granting me this amazing opportunity to share my wedding designs; Christine Doyle for her unique vision in planning the overall concept of the book; my wonderful editor, Jessica Gordon, for her creative guidance and hard work; my "wild and crazy" photographer, Christine Polomsky, for making the photo shoot such a blast; and Leigh Ann Lentz and Mary Barnes Clark for their lovely design work. As always, it has been a pleasure working with all of you.

My special thanks also goes out to all of you "picture-perfect" couples, Michael and Karen, Brent and Melissa, Mike and Jean, and Anne and Thomas, for inspiring me with your gorgeous wedding photos. And let's not forget little "Sophie Bear" who was my inspiration in designing the flower girl projects.

Preparing for the photo shoot was a breeze thanks to the companies who so generously contributed supplies to re-create the projects in this book: Delta Technical Coatings, Inc.; Loew-Cornell, Inc.; Plaid Enterprises, Inc.; and DMD Industries.

And last, but certainly not least, my sincere appreciation goes out to my family, especially my husband, Tom; Pops and Laurie; Auntie Mary; and Michael and Karen, for your continued encouragement and support. And in special memory of my dear mother, Nettie, I thank her with all of my heart for helping me to create the wedding of my dreams over twenty years ago.

Table of Contents

Sweet Sentiments 36

Let's Celebrate! 50

Happily Ever After 66

Forever
in our
Hearts
Kelly Grondin
Johnny R.

Introduction

A wedding is one of life's most memorable and joyful occasions. It's the perfect opportunity to create a one-of-a-kind celebration that your guests will be buzzing about for years to come! So forget the typical "cookie-cutter" wedding drenched in the same old worn-out details...with *Crafting a Dream Wedding*, you'll discover a wide variety of creative ideas and handcrafted wedding touches that will make your special day unlike any other.

Handcrafting your own personalized wedding touches is also cost-effective and enables you to spend quality time with close friends and family members as you include them in the joyful preparation for your special day. You'll have more control over the finished details, and your wedding celebration will become more meaningful knowing that some or all of your decorations, favors and keepsakes were crafted and shared from the heart with love and happiness.

Whether you're the blushing bride, a close friend or relative of the happy couple, or an honored member of the wedding party, *Crafting a Dream Wedding* will give you a multitude of ideas for planning every aspect of this glorious occasion. The five themed chapters will give you plenty of fresh and unique ideas for everything from bridal shower and pre-wedding parties to special touches and decorative accents for an unforgettable ceremony and wedding reception. And for capturing those enchanting storybook memories, there are lots of picture-perfect ideas for creating photographic keepsakes that you're sure to cherish for years to come. The pages are brimming with fun and festive favors and gorgeous gift ideas that will take you from "Once Upon a Time" to "Happily Ever After."

And like most brides who are short on time, you'll appreciate our quick and easy crafting techniques for creating projects that even novice crafters can make with ease. If you're a bride with a fun and funky style, you'll love our festive candy bouquets and centerpieces and our nontraditional Tasty Treat Table Numbers and miniature guest books. If you're dreaming of a more traditional and romantic-style wedding, you'll delight in crafting our exquisite ring pillow, unity candles and Victorian-inspired floral petal cones.

No matter what wedding style you choose, from traditionally romantic and elegant to a more modern and contemporary theme, with *Crafting a Dream Wedding* you're sure to find projects that perfectly capture the essence of your fairytale wedding. And as you browse through page after page of these stylish touches, remember that there is always room to adapt each project to reflect your own personal taste and color scheme. Let your imagination soar as you plan the wedding of your dreams.

Basic Materials

Before you begin crafting the elegant wedding projects in this book, you'll need to make sure you have some basic crafting supplies on hand. As you create each project, you'll need a variety of readily available supplies such as scissors, a ruler and hot glue gun, acrylic paints, brushes, and floral and papercrafting supplies. You can find any additional items at your local craft retailers.

General Painting Supplies

For the painting projects in this book, I use the American Painter Series brushes from Loew-Cornell and Delta Ceramcoat acrylic paints. Other essential supplies include découpage medium, spray and brush-on varnish and crackle medium to create different surface finishes. I also use a couple of extra tools, such as an old toothbrush and pieces of sponge, to create different painted effects.

- **Loew-Cornell American Painter Series brushes,** including: no.10 shader (4300), ½" (13mm) and ¾" (19mm) wash brushes (4550) and no. 10 flat (4250); and 1" (25mm) and 2" (51mm) foam brushes (755) are useful for basecoating larger areas and for applying the découpage and crackle mediums.
- **Delta Ceramcoat acrylic paints** are perfect for painting on wood, papier-maché, terra cotta and other craft surfaces. (Refer to the individual project instructions for suggested colors.)
- **Delta Ceramcoat matte interior spray varnish** and **matte interior (brush-on) varnish** add a clear, protective finish to your decorative painting projects.
- **Delta Ceramcoat satin découpage medium** is a thick, spreadable glue and sealer that dries clear and can be used to adhere paper items to various surfaces.
- **Delta Ceramcoat crackle medium** is applied over a dry basecoat of paint to create an aged surface.
- An **old toothbrush** is used to spatter paint.
- **Small pieces of sponge** are used to basecoat and create a textured appearance on painted surfaces. (I use the compressed sheets of sponge that expand when moistened in water.)
- A **brush basin** or **water tub** is essential for maintaining clean brushes.
- **Wax paper** makes a cost-effective palette for painting and sponge-painting.
- A **blow-dryer** helps speed up the drying process.
- **Paper towels** are essential for cleanup and for drying brushes in between rinsing.

Supplies for Working with Wire

For a few projects in this book, you'll need to do some basic wire work, like twisting, cutting and shaping wire. Crafting items out of wire and/or adding wire touches to other types of projects is a simple way to create a sophisticated look that's also functional.

- **Wire cutters** are stronger than scissors and are used for cutting all kinds of wire.
- **Needle-nose pliers** have flat metal pincers and are used for gripping wire and twisting it into different shapes.
- **Decorative gold and silver wire** comes in all different gauges (from very fine to thick) and can be twisted into any desired shape.
- **Wooden dowels and thin paintbrush handles** are useful for curling wire stems and for adding curlicues.

From top to bottom: Loew-Cornell paintbrushes; (from left to right) needle-nose pliers and wire cutters; (from left to right) Delta Ceramcoat acrylic paints, crackle medium, découpage medium and interior spray varnish

Papercrafting Supplies

Many of the projects in this book use scrapbook paper and other papercrafting supplies and embellishments, such as those listed below.

- A **ruler** is useful for measuring, scoring and even for tearing paper in a straight line. Deckle-edge rulers are also available for tearing paper in a decorative design.
- A **craft knife** is great for making small cuts and precise lines.
- **Scissors** are essential for any crafting project.
- A **hot glue gun** and **hot glue sticks** are used to adhere trims onto your papercrafts.
- A **glue pen** is a small pen-shaped glue dispenser with a narrow applicator to give you optimum control.
- **Double-sided tape** is great for holding paper together seamlessly and securely.
- **Decorative-edge scissors** let you cut paper in any number of decorative designs.
- **Scrapbook paper and scrapbook embellishments** add the perfect finishing touch to your papercraft projects.
- A **bone folder** is a smooth, flat tool with one rounded end and one pointed end used to score paper and to create crisp folds.

Supplies for Making Floral Arrangements

All weddings must have flowers, of course, and many of the projects in this book incorporate floral arrangements into their designs. You'll need just a few simple materials and tools to create beautiful floral arrangements.

- **Pruning shears** are sharp cutting tools used to cut flowers off of stems.
- **Artificial flowers** come in every conceivable variety and color scheme to match your wedding theme.
- **Floral wire** is sturdy wire used to bind flowers together in specific arrangements.
- **Floral tape** is a special kind of stretchy adhesive that is used to hold floral stems together.
- **Green sheet moss** is found with flower-arranging supplies and is often used to cover floral foam shapes.
- **Floral foam bricks** and **foam heart** and **ball shapes** are used for anchoring floral arrangements.
- A **sharp knife** is used to cut floral foam bricks.
- A **hot glue gun** and **glue sticks** are essential tools for most floral crafts.

Crafty Bride Tip

You can add a fresh and modern look to your wedding touches using the endless supply of paper products and scrapbook trims available at your local craft or paper supply store. I use an assortment of scrapbook paper, stickers, floral napkins, ivory cardstock, tags, place cards, bookmarks and three-dimensional scrapbook and paper embellishments, to name a few. Alphabet stickers are also a great way to personalize your creative paper designs.

You can also choose from a vast array of romantic trims such as satin and sheer ribbons, strings of pearls, beads and jewels, lace and tulle, miniature paper roses, beaded and pearl flower accents… the list goes on and on. Let your own unique style guide you as you choose trims that complement your wedding theme.

Clockwise from top left: foam sphere, bone folder, beaded flower trims and artificial floral trims, floral foam brick and ribbons

Terms & Techniques

Before you begin to craft your dream wedding, take a few minutes to familiarize yourself with some of the basic crafting terms and techniques used in this book. Because not all brides are avid crafters, the projects in this book require only basic crafting skills. Once you've mastered these fun and simple crafting techniques, you can keep using them long after the wedding to create a variety of home décor projects to fill your love nest with elegance and style.

Painting Terms & Techniques

Many of the projects in this book involve a few simple painting techniques. You'll create wonderful painted effects with spattering, antiquing, sponge painting and crackle techniques. Painting your projects is a fast and easy way to put your own personal stamp on the items you make. Refer to the techniques below as you begin painting projects for your dream wedding.

Basecoating: Using a flat brush, apply at least two coats of paint to ensure solid coverage. Be sure to allow the paint to dry in between coats. If you like, you can use a blow-dryer to speed up the drying process.

Spattering or "Fly Specking": For this technique, use an old toothbrush to apply tiny specks of paint onto the surface area. Although some designers prefer to thin their paint with water first (approximately ⅔ paint to ⅓ water), I prefer to simply moisten the toothbrush bristles, then dip the toothbrush into a pool of paint. Remove the excess paint onto a piece of paper towel, then run your finger across the ends of the bristles, holding the toothbrush over the area to be spattered.

Antiquing: Use this technique to create a rich, timeworn look on any painted surface. Thin a small dab of dark brown paint with water, then apply the wash onto the surface, gradually adding more coats to deepen the color to the desired shade. There are also antiquing mediums available in a variety of shades that are specifically designed for this painting technique.

Sponge Painting: A small piece of dampened sponge can be used to basecoat some of the projects (such as the Wedding Memories Time Capsule [page 76] and the glass pot base of the Floral Heart Cake Topper [page 56]). Simply dip the dampened sponge into a pool of paint and apply it onto the surface of your project. It's important to remember that this type of painting should be done with a damp, not wet, sponge, so be sure to squeeze the excess water from the sponge. If your sponge is too wet, the paint will bleed onto your surface.

Crackle Technique: Delta Ceramcoat's crackle medium is a great way to give an instant aged or vintage look to your wedding projects. Once you've applied your basecoat color, you simply apply an even coat of the crackle medium over the painted surface and allow it to air dry until tacky. The amount of drying time can vary anywhere from 15 to 40 minutes depending on the humidity in the room where you're working and the thickness of the coat you apply. Once you apply the top coat, the crackle effect will appear almost instantaneously.

Painting Tips

- Cover your work surface with wax paper to make a cost-effective palette for your painting and sponge-painting techniques.
- Use a blow-dryer to speed up the drying process.
- Have a brush basin or container of clean water handy to rinse your brushes. Don't allow the paint to dry on the bristles.
- When spattering, always test the consistency of the paint before applying it to your finished project.
- The more water you add to your paint or to the bristles of your toothbrush for spattering, the larger and more transparent the spatters will be.

Additional Techniques

For some of the projects in this book, you may be working with different kinds of materials for the first time. Take a moment to look over the following techniques for working with paper, wire and other mediums.

Découpage: Any bride can become a "découpage diva" using this quick and easy crafting technique. Using Delta's découpage medium, you can decorate almost any type of surface with a variety of romantic paper accents. In this book, I show you how to découpage with scrapbook paper, floral napkins, tissue paper, stickers and even cloth doilies. You can also découpage your favorite photos to personalize your one-of-a-kind wedding décor and keepsakes.

Découpage Tips

Using the découpage technique, you can preserve a variety of paper motifs from your wedding story while creating one-of-a-kind collage keepsakes and home décor accents. Just a few sources of inspiration include:

- copies of wedding and honeymoon photos
- engagement and wedding newspaper announcements
- wedding napkins
- wedding invitation and program
- paper motifs cut from your shower or wedding cards
- tissue paper or gift wrap from your shower and wedding
- ticket stubs, brochures, receipts and other memorabilia from your honeymoon vacation
- copy of your wedding certificate
- old love letters (or stamps and postmarks cut from their envelopes)

Bending & Shaping Wire: Use needle-nose pliers to curl the ends of your wire stems into coiled shapes to hold photos, place cards and menu cards. To curl a piece of wire for a decorative touch, wrap the wire piece tightly around a wooden dowel or paintbrush handle.

Applying Rub-On Decals & Stencils: There are many brands of rub-on decals and stencils available, so be sure to refer to the individual manufacturer's instructions, as they vary from brand to brand. For example, Plaid's FolkArt One Stroke Decals (which I use on the Enchanted Garden File Box [page 20] and Wedding Keepsake Candle [page 72]) are applied using a dampened sponge, whereas the Imperial Instant Stencils (which I use on the Love in Full Bloom Centerpiece [page 14]) are rubbed onto the surface using a plastic applicator.

Scoring & Folding Paper: When folding heavier-weight paper into cards, tags, miniature guest books or photo albums, it's much easier if you use a ruler and bone folder to score and press the creases of the folds. Check out the Wedding Wishes Guest Books (page 52) for step-by-step photos illustrating these papercrafting techniques.

Transferring Patterns & Creating Templates: To transfer the patterns on page 77, begin by using a pencil to trace the desired pattern onto a sheet of transparent tracing paper. Insert a piece of gray transfer paper in between the traced pattern and a piece of lightweight cardboard or posterboard. Using a pencil, a ball-point pen or a stylus, retrace the pattern, transferring it onto the surface of the lightweight cardboard or posterboard. Once the cardboard shape is cut out, use it as a template by tracing around the outer edges with a pencil.

Lisa
Merrie
Kim & Mike
Save the Date
07·22·0

Once Upon a Time

It's a time of celebration—your fairytale romance has blossomed, and you and your prince charming are ready to plan the wedding of your dreams. Make your wedding planning experience as unique as your love affair by adding the small, personal touches that will make your day truly unforgettable.

Begin your wedding preparations by sending your future guests a charming Save-the-Date Bookmark Card (page 18). As you begin to plan all the dreamy details, you'll want to craft the exquisite Wedding Dreams Organizer (page 19) to keep all of your wedding ideas and information at your fingertips. The Enchanted Garden File Box (page 20) is perfect for storing your guest reply cards and can play double duty as a charming recipe box to brighten your kitchen décor.

The pre-wedding celebrations are a memorable part of every wedding, and this chapter provides a great selection of ideas that allow your personal touch and creative style to shine through. Your bridal attendants will delight in receiving their very own Bridesmaids' Fortune Bouquet favors (page 17) at their special luncheon. Your bridal shower guests will be thrilled to pick their very own seed packet favor from the Love in Full Bloom watering can centerpiece (page 14). And as the big day finally approaches, let's not forget the wedding rehearsal celebration. Your entrance down the aisle will be extra sweet as you carry a handcrafted candy bouquet of yummy lollipops and heavenly chocolate hearts (page 22).

No doubt the months to follow will be a whirlwind of activity as you begin your journey into wedded bliss. Just remember to enjoy the ride and to cherish the time spent with family and friends each step of the way. Happy planning!

Love in Full Bloom

Centerpiece

Shower the bride-to-be in true style with this fresh-from-the-garden seed packet centerpiece. Accented with dainty paper doilies and romantic ribbon trims, this lovely bouquet of seed packet favors is planted in a charming watering can base ready for picking by the bridal shower guests. Both beautiful and functional, the seed packet blooms will be a joyful reminder of the couple's everlasting love.

❤ Materials List ❤

Watering Can Base:

- metal watering can, 7" (18cm) high x 5" (13cm) in diameter
- floral decals or rub-on stencils and plastic applicator
  LARGE FLORAL DESIGNS FROM IMPERIAL INSTANT STENCILS
- two floral foam bricks
- green sheet moss
- assorted artificial flowers (with stems removed) in shades of pink, purple, yellow and white
- sprigs of artificial baby's breath
- $1\frac{1}{2}$" (4cm) lilac floral satin ribbon
- pruning shears
- sharp knife
- hot glue gun and glue sticks
- scissors
- ruler

"Love in Full Bloom" Tag and Name Tags:

- dusty pink or lavender tag with metal punched hole, $2\frac{1}{2}$" x 4" (6cm x 10cm)
- white cardstock
- miniature floral stickers
- alphabet stickers
- curling ribbon
- $\frac{1}{8}$" (3mm) hole punch
- decorative-edge scissors

Seed Packet Favors:

- assorted flower seed packets
- 4" (10cm) white paper doilies (2–3 doily thickness for each favor)
- 12" (30cm) wooden dowels, $\frac{3}{16}$" (5mm) in diameter
- Delta Ceramcoat acrylic paint in Lisa Pink, Dusty Plum and White
- Delta Ceramcoat matte interior spray varnish
- $\frac{5}{16}$" (8mm) sheer pink and lavender ribbon
- miniature self-adhesive paper roses ($\frac{1}{2}$" [1cm]) in pink, yellow and white
- curling ribbon to accent handle (optional)
- glue pen
- paintbrush and general painting supplies

Crafty Bride Tip

A plastic ruler can also be used as an applicator to apply the type of stencil used here. However, always refer to the package instructions before beginning. Other kinds of stencils are applied using a damp sponge or cloth instead of a plastic applicator.

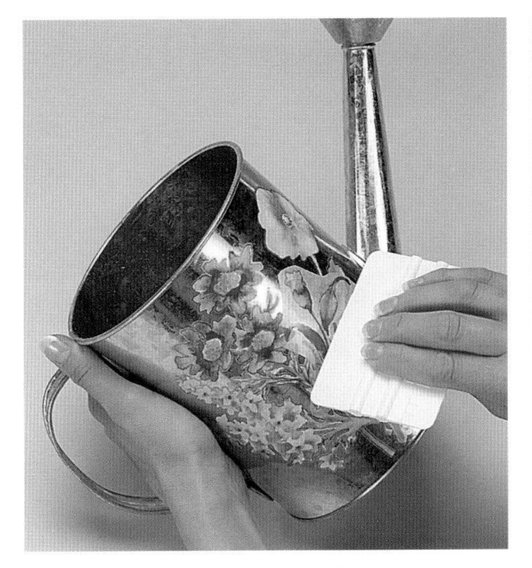

1 Apply Rub-On Decals
Using scissors, cut out the desired floral motifs from the stencil sheet, leaving a small border around the images to make it easy to transfer the designs. Lay the cutout flowers on your work surface in a pleasing arrangement. Remove the protective backing from the first stencil that you wish to apply and place it on the watering can. Adhere the stencil by rubbing the surface evenly with a plastic applicator. Slowly peel away the top clear layer. If the design is not fully transferred, you can reposition the top layer and continue to rub. Repeat for each stencil.

2 Insert Floral Foam Base
Use a sharp knife to cut the floral foam bricks to fit inside the watering can. Cut additional smaller pieces of foam to fill in any gaps. Hot glue the foam pieces to secure them inside the watering can. Add more hot glue between the seams of the bricks to stabilize them.

3 Add Sheet Moss
Hot glue the green sheet moss on top of the floral bricks to completely conceal the base.

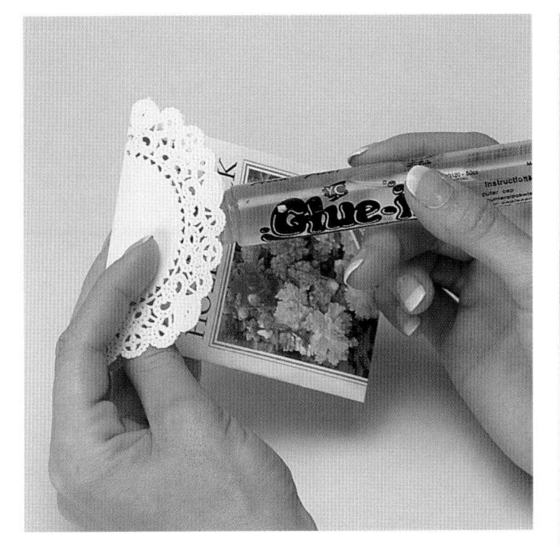

4 Glue Doilies onto Seed Packets
Using a thickness of two to three doilies, fold them in half as one and glue them onto the top of a seed packet using a glue pen. (It's preferable to use two to three doilies stuck together for the seed packet favors because one doily by itself is too transparent.) Repeat for each seed packet.

5 Glue Trims onto Seed Packets
Tie a 10" (25cm) length of 5/16" (8mm) lavender or pink ribbon into a bow, and trim ends to desired length. Hot glue the bow onto the doily and hot glue a paper rose onto the center of the bow. Repeat for each seed packet favor.

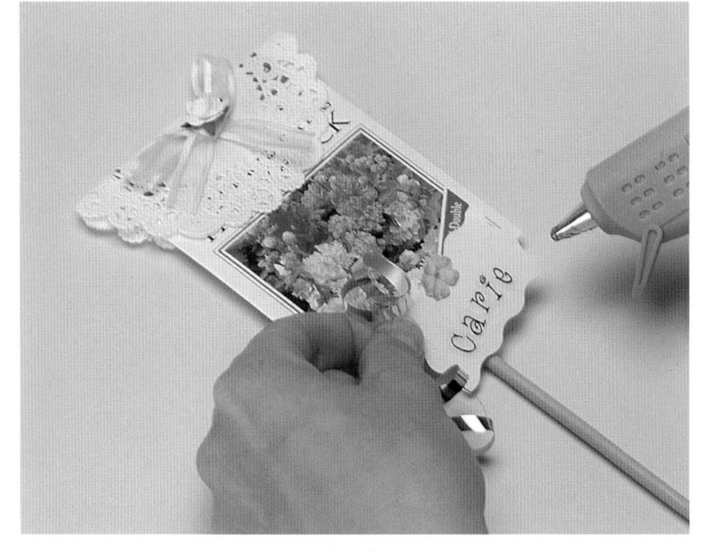

6 *Paint Dowel Rods and Adhere Seed Packets*

Paint each dowel rod with either Lisa Pink, Dusty Plum or White. When they are dry, apply the matte spray varnish. Gently turn the seed packet over so that the back side is facing up. Apply a line of hot glue to the top 4" (10cm) of the dowel rod (or the length of the seed packet) and adhere it to the back center of the seed packet. Repeat for each seed packet. Create name tags by cutting out 1¼" x 2" (3cm x 5cm) pieces of white cardstock with decorative-edge scissors. Spell out a name on the tag with letter stickers and adhere a miniature flower sticker to accent the top of each tag. Punch a small hole in the top corner of the tag and tie on a piece of curling ribbon. Hot glue the tags onto the top of each dowel rod directly beneath the seed packet.

7 *Place Favors in Watering Can*

Arrange the seed packet favors in the watering can by pushing the dowel rods through the sheet moss and into the floral foam base. Be sure to arrange the seed packet favors at different heights and angles to create a pleasing bouquet effect.

8 *Glue Floral Trims onto Base*

Hot glue the artificial flowers and baby's breath sprigs onto the sheet moss so that they surround the dowel rod stems of the seed packet favors.

9 *Add Bow and Tag to Watering Can*

Tie a bow around the handle of the watering can with a 24" (61cm) length of the 1½" (4cm) wide floral satin ribbon. If desired, add a "Love in Full Bloom" tag to the handle. Cut a piece of white cardstock to approximately 2" x 3" (5cm x 8cm) with decorative-edge scissors. Glue the rectangular piece of cardstock onto the tag and spell out "Love in Full Bloom" with black alphabet stickers. Accent the tag with three miniature floral stickers and tie it onto the handle with the curling ribbon.

Bridesmaids' Fortune *Bouquets*

Play fortuneteller at your bridesmaids' luncheon with these charming floral bouquet favors. Each individually crafted bouquet is personalized with a printed fortune tag that you dream up for each of your bridal attendants. The tags are then accented with a charm that best symbolizes the future destiny of each lady. Use the bouquet favors as place cards at each table setting or in a crystal vase for a unique centerpiece idea.

Materials List

- single artificial rose stems with leaves
- artificial cream hydrangea blooms with berry clusters
- green floral tape
- 9" (23cm) tulle circles
- 1/4" (6mm) ivory ribbon
- 5/8" (2cm) sheer pink wired ribbon
- hot glue gun and glue sticks
- scissors
- ruler

Decorative Tags:

- white or ivory cardstock
- various charms (to complement each fortune)
- alphabet stickers
- 1/8" (3mm) ivory ribbon
- 1/8" (3mm) hole punch
- decorative-edge scissors

1. Using the green floral tape, attach several hydrangea blooms (with berries) around the top front and sides of the rose stem.

2. Gather a tulle circle in the center to form a fan-shaped cluster, then hot glue the tulle onto the back of the bouquet. Hot glue additional hydrangea blooms to conceal the glued part of the tulle.

3. Cut a 16" to 18" (41cm to 46cm) piece of the 1/4" (6mm) ivory ribbon and hot glue it around the length of the stem.

4. Tie a bow with a 16" (41cm) length of the 5/8" (2cm) sheer pink ribbon. Trim the ends of the bow to the desired length, then hot glue the bow onto the top of the stem.

5. For the tag, use decorative-edge scissors to cut a small folded piece of white or ivory cardstock. Punch two tiny holes into the top of the tag, then thread a length of the 1/8" (3mm) ivory ribbon through the holes, string the charm onto the ribbon and tie a bow to secure it. Use alphabet stickers to personalize the tag, then write the bridesmaid's special fortune on the inside. For example, if you have a bridesmaid who loves to travel, you might write a fortune such as, "You are a traveler at heart—many journeys stretch before you." Choose a suitcase or an airplane charm to attach to the tag and the theme is complete. For a bridesmaid who is embarking on a new career or who is advancing in an established one, you might choose a fortune such as, "A life of excitement and fulfillment awaits you." Attach a briefcase charm to her tag to complete it. For the final touch, hot glue the back of the tag onto the rose stem. Repeat steps 1–5 for each favor.

Save-the-Date
Bookmark Card

Once you've set the date for your dream wedding, you'll want to spread the news with our charming Save-the-Date Bookmark Cards. Simply purchase the bookmarks and blank note cards in bulk, then decorate them using an assortment of scrapbook papers, stickers and ribbon trims. These decorated bookmarks are a fun yet functional way to announce your engagement and to remind friends and family of your special date.

Kim & Mike

Save the Date

07 · 22 · 06

Materials List

- large folded note cards, 5 1/8" x 7 3/8" (13cm x 19cm)
- pre-packaged blank bookmarks, 2 1/2" x 6" (6cm x 15cm), or cut your own out of heavy white or ivory cardstock
- embossed vellum scrapbook paper
  K&Company's Daisy Printed Embossed Vellum
- dimensional and flat scrapbook stickers
  K&Company's Daisy Stickers
- alphabet and number stickers
- 5/16" (8mm) sheer yellow ribbon
- vellum tape (or double-sided tape)
- hot glue gun and glue sticks
- craft utility knife
- pencil
- scissors
- ruler

1. To save time, purchase bulk quantities of pre-packaged bookmarks. If you prefer to make your own, cut them out of heavy white or ivory cardstock to the dimensions as listed in the Materials List.

2. Trace around the bookmark onto the printed vellum paper, then cut the 2 1/2" x 6" (6cm x 15cm) piece of vellum out using scissors. Attach the vellum piece onto the bookmark using the vellum tape or double-sided tape.

3. Use the alphabet and number stickers to add your names and wedding date onto the bookmark. Center your names at the top and the wedding date directly along the bottom edge. Decorate the center of the bookmark with the flat and dimensional stickers as desired.

4. Cut a 6" (15cm) length of the 5/16" (8mm) yellow ribbon. Form a loop shape, then hot glue the ends of the ribbon onto the back of the bookmark.

5. Place the bookmark on the front of the card toward the left-hand side. When the bookmark is in the desired position, use a pencil to lightly trace around the top left and bottom right corners of the bookmark onto the card. Open the card so it lies flat, then use a craft knife to cut two diagonal slits in each corner, using the pencil marks as a reference. Erase the pencil lines.

6. Insert the bookmark into the corner slits.

7. Use alphabet stickers to spell out "Save the Date" on the right side of the card, and then accent the card with the desired stickers for the finishing touch.

Wedding Dreams *Organizer*

With just one visit to your local scrapbook and office supply stores, you'll have everything you need to create this enchanting organizer. You'll use a variety of scrapbook paper and three-dimensional trims to give this inexpensive cardboard file folder a quick and easy makeover. It's perfect for keeping all of your wedding information at your fingertips. And after your wedding, it's pretty enough to use as a keepsake folder to store all your wedding planning mementos.

Materials List

- accordion file folder, 12" x 9½" (30cm x 24cm)
- two pieces of heavy flat or embossed scrapbook paper, 12" x 12" (30cm x 30cm)
  K&Company's Beaded Flower Printed Embossed Paper and Juliana Muscari Printed Flat Paper
- scrapbook borders
  K&Company's Juliana Lilac Borders
- dimensional scrapbook stickers
  K&Company's Juliana Dragonfly & Flowers
- 5/16" (8mm) sheer lavender ribbon
- alphabet stickers
- seven miniature silk lavender flowers (with stems removed)
- glue pen
- hot glue gun and glue sticks
- standard hole punch
- scissors
- pencil

1. Use a pencil to trace around the edge of the accordion file folder onto the two pieces of scrapbook paper. Cut out each piece of scrapbook paper with scissors.

2. Use a glue pen to apply the scrapbook papers onto the front and back of the file folder. (I use the embossed paper on the front and the flat paper on the back.) Use your fingers to firmly rub along the surface of the paper to smooth out any wrinkles or creases.

3. Apply the two scrapbook borders onto the front of the folder, one along the very bottom and the other just over halfway up.

4. Punch a single hole through the front and back of the folder at the top center. Insert a 20" (51cm) piece of lavender ribbon through the holes and tie a bow to secure the opening shut.

5. Apply the alphabet stickers to spell out "Wedding Dreams" along the top border.

6. Apply the dimensional dragonfly and flower stickers as desired.

7. Hot glue the seven miniature silk flowers onto the file folder, three along each side and one just beneath the lavender bow.

Enchanted Garden *File Box*

This enchanting garden treasure makes a perfect shower gift for the bride-to-be. For a personal touch, ask each shower guest to bring a favorite recipe, then insert the recipe cards into the box to make a memorable keepsake. Or the box can be used as a wedding organizer to file guest reply cards and to store wedding-related phone numbers and contact information.

Crafty Bride Tip

Before applying the crackle medium, be sure to read the manufacturer's directions. Drying time for crackle medium can vary from 15 to 40 minutes, depending on the thickness of the coat you apply and the humidity of the room where you're working. I find that a drying time of about 25 to 30 minutes works best for a medium coat. If you've never worked with crackle medium before, it's a good idea to practice first before applying it to your final project. Once you have the technique mastered, you can use it on all sorts of projects to create a fashionable vintage look.

Materials List

- wooden file box, approximately 6½" (17cm) wide x 4½" (11cm) deep x 4" (10cm) high
- Delta Ceramcoat acrylic paint in Wedgwood Green and Light Ivory
- Delta Ceramcoat matte interior varnish
- Delta Ceramcoat crackle medium
- decal with leaves and flowers
  PLAID FOLKART ONE STROKE DECAL, FLORAL VINES COLLECTION
- three 5" (13cm) pieces of miniature artificial ivy garland
- three green artificial berry sprigs
- artificial floral trims with stems removed (three white daisies and three miniature yellow flowers)
- 1½" (4cm) miniature bird's nest
- three ½" (1cm) miniature plastic speckled eggs
- 1½" (4cm) miniature green bird
- old toothbrush (for spattering)
- small piece of sponge
- paintbrushes and general painting supplies
- hot glue gun and glue sticks
- scissors

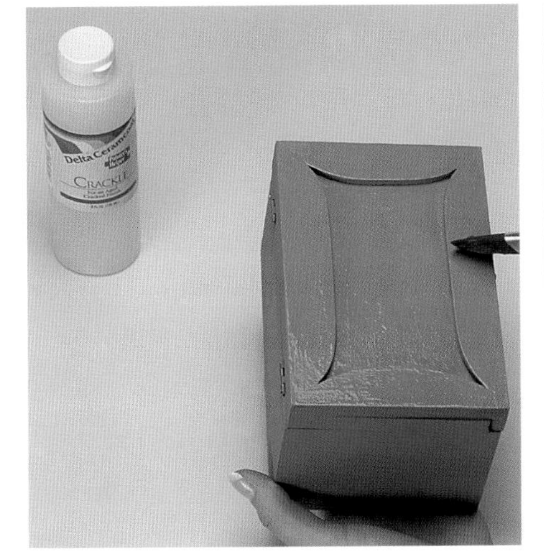

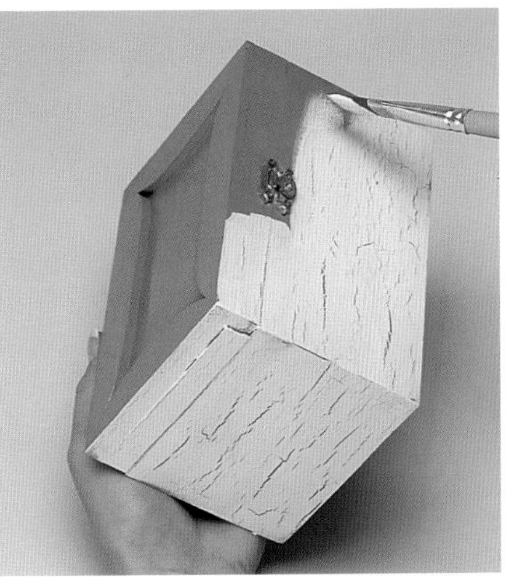

1 *Apply Crackle Medium*
Basecoat the entire box with Wedgwood Green. Allow the paint to dry. Following the manufacturer's instructions, apply an even coat of the crackle medium to the top and two sides of the box. (Applying the crackle technique in two stages allows you to handle the box more easily.)

2 *Paint Box with Top Coat*
Let the crackle medium dry until tacky (about 25 to 30 minutes for a medium coat). Apply a light, even top coat of the Light Ivory paint over the crackle medium. Allow the box to dry. The aged, crackle effect will appear within minutes. Repeat steps 1 and 2 for the bottom and remaining two sides.

3 *Spatter Box*
When the box is completely dry, use an old toothbrush to spatter the outside with Wedgwood Green and the inside with Light Ivory. Allow the paint to dry.

4 *Apply Floral Decal to Box*
Apply the matte varnish to the entire box and allow it to dry. Choose the decal you would like to use and cut it out, leaving a small border around the image. Following the manufacturer's instructions, gently peel off the transparent layer and adhere the image to the front of the box by firmly pressing it onto the surface. Using a small piece of dampened sponge, moisten the entire surface of the decal. After about 60 seconds, gently peel off the white paper coating. With the damp sponge, gently smooth the decal onto the surface and allow it to dry.

5 *Add Trims to Top of Box*
To protect the surface of the floral decal, apply another coat of the matte interior varnish. Allow it to dry. Hot glue the three pieces of miniature ivy garland and the three berry sprigs onto the top of the box. Then glue on the artificial floral trims. Finish the box by gluing the three plastic eggs into the bird's nest and adhering the filled nest and the bird onto the top of the box.

Sweet Lollipop
Rehearsal Bouquet

Your rehearsal ceremony will be extra sweet when you carry this colorful candy bouquet down the aisle. A fun alternative to the traditional ribbons-and-bows rehearsal bouquet, this edible version is fashioned from yummy lollipops, heavenly chocolate hearts and a festive array of package trims. After the ceremony, the bouquet can play double duty as an edible centerpiece for the kids' table. Or you can save it for the wedding reception as a memorable throw-away bouquet.

Materials List

- white plastic bouquet holder with a foam insert and a 9" (23cm) lace collar trim
- two white curly ribbon clusters with pearl string accents (buy them ready-made or make your own by purchasing the white curling ribbon and pearl strings separately)
- white tulle package bow
- 2½" (6cm) sheer white ribbon with pearl beaded trim
- assortment of lollipops and foil-wrapped chocolate hearts
- hot glue gun and glue sticks
- scissors
- ruler

1. Hot glue the foil-wrapped chocolate hearts around the inner edge of the lace trim collar on the bouquet holder. Be sure to save three chocolates to accent the center of the bouquet.

2. Insert the stems of the lollipops into the foam base in a pleasing arrangement. To make them extra secure, you can add a dab of hot glue onto the stem of each lollipop before inserting it.

3. Hot glue the tulle package bow in the center of the bouquet.

4. Hot glue the clusters of white curly ribbon and pearl accents onto the bouquet.

5. Cut 40" (102cm) of the 2½" (6cm) wide sheer white ribbon and tie it into a bow. Hot glue the bow onto the top of the handle.

6. For the finishing touch, hot glue three chocolate hearts to accent the center of the bouquet.

Mint

Shower the bride-to-be with these tasty Mint Umbrella Favors. Simply fill a disposable pastry bag with dessert mints and insert a lollipop stick for a handle. For the finishing touch, add miniature paper flower accents, satin bows and pearl beaded trim. To coordinate with this charming favor idea, use umbrella-themed shower decorations and invitations.

Materials List

- 12" (30cm) disposable pastry bags
- dessert mints
- 4mm pink pearl string
- 1/4" (6mm) pale green ribbon
- miniature pink paper flower trims (four for each favor)
- 6" (15cm) lollipop sticks (one for each favor)
- transparent tape
- hot glue gun and glue sticks
- decorative-edge scissors
- scissors
- ruler

1. Use decorative-edge scissors to cut around the top edge of each pastry bag.
2. Fill each pastry bag with mints, then insert a lollipop stick into the center of the mints. Use a piece of transparent tape to secure the top of the bag closed. Repeat for each favor.
3. Cut three 5" (13cm) pieces of the 4mm pearl string for each umbrella favor. Hot glue the ends of each pearl string to form a loop, then glue the three loops at the base of the stem.
4. Tie a 10" (25cm) length of the 1/4" (6mm) pale green ribbon into a bow. Trim the ends of the bow to the desired length. Hot glue the bow onto the center of the pearl loops. Repeat for each favor.
5. Hot glue the miniature paper flower trims onto the favors, one onto the center of each bow and three spaced evenly along the front of each pastry bag.

Here Comes the Bride

After months of anticipation and careful planning, it's time to make your grand entrance down the aisle. Adding special handcrafted touches to your wedding day will truly celebrate the love you share for one another and for the family and friends who have supported you every step of the way.

In this chapter, you'll learn how to personalize your ceremony with heartwarming decorating ideas. Best of all, these dreamy décor ideas and ceremony accents can be used even after you say "I do" to decorate the reception or to be given as thoughtful gifts. Or you may prefer to keep these enchanting wedding touches as keepsakes to cherish for years to come.

For your littlest attendant, you can craft an enchanting floral headpiece and coordinating rose petal basket (page 28). For a truly romantic touch, it's "sew" easy to create a sweet ring pillow (page 26) and matching heart sachet from lacy linen doilies and a few crafty trims. You'll also find many creative ideas for crafting flower-filled cornucopias, unity candles and even a "charming" mother's corsage (page 33).

The Forever in Our Hearts Memory Bouquet (page 34) is a wonderfully unique way to incorporate those dearly departed loved ones into your ceremony. As you exchange your vows, you can pay a heartwarming tribute to special friends and family members by including favorite photos in the wire accent stems of the floral bouquet.

After you've said your "I do's" and as you make your way down the aisle, your guests can enjoy the time-honored tradition of tossing rose petals from the delightful Victorian-inspired paper cones (page 30). As you jump into your getaway vehicle, you can now breathe a sigh of relief…for it's off to the reception to dance the night away!

Romantic *Ring Pillow*

Add a touch of romantic elegance to your wedding ceremony with this exquisite ring pillow. Hand-stitched doilies stuffed with fiberfill make this project "sew" easy to create! And with its classic design, it can serve double duty as a stylish accent pillow to complement your bedroom décor. As a charming variation, individually crafted heart pillows make lovely keepsake sachets to give away as gifts or favors. Simply add a ribbon hanger and tuck sprigs of lavender inside for a fragrant touch.

Materials List

- two round scalloped-edge white linen doilies, approximately 10" (25cm)
- two heart-shaped white linen doilies, approximately 5½" (14cm)
- nine ¾" (2cm) miniature artificial lavender roses (with stems removed)
- seven ¾" (2cm) pearl flower trims (with stems removed)
- ⅝" (2cm) sheer lavender wired ribbon
- ⅛" (3mm) white ribbon
- sewing needle and white thread
- polyester fiberfill
- iron
- hot glue gun and glue sticks
- scissors
- ruler

Dream Idea

Heart Sachet

To craft coordinating heart sachets, follow the same steps for making the small heart pillow, adding sprigs of lavender into the sachet pillow for a fragrant touch, if desired. Tie the ends of a 15" (38cm) length of ⅛" (3mm) white ribbon into the top left and right sides of the scalloped-edge trim to create a hanger. Tie two bows using 9" (23cm) lengths of the white ribbon and glue the bows onto each end of the hanger. To finish, hot glue a lavender beaded pearl flower trim on top of each bow.

1 *Sew Doilies Together, Stuff Pillow*
Iron the doilies to remove any wrinkles or creases. Position the two round doilies back to back. Use a sewing needle and white thread to stitch the doilies together around the inner edge of the scalloped lace trim, leaving an opening of approximately 3" to 4" (8cm to 10cm) for stuffing. Stuff the pillow with fiberfill.

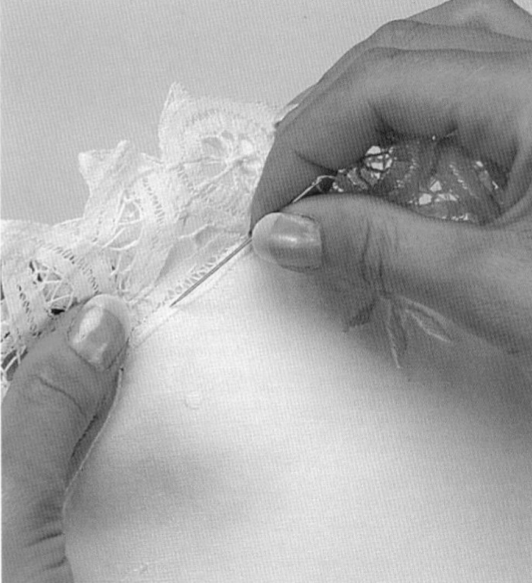

2 *Stitch Opening Shut*
Use the sewing needle and white thread to stitch the opening in the pillow closed.

Crafty Bride Tip

Use a paintbrush handle to stuff the fiberfill into hard-to-reach areas.

3 *Attach Small Pillow, Add Trims*
Repeat steps 1 and 2 for the smaller heart pillow, leaving a 2" (5cm) opening for stuffing. Hot glue the heart pillow onto the top center of the larger round pillow. Hot glue the trims around the inside of the lace edge of the round pillow, alternating between the lavender rosebuds and the pearl flower trims. To ensure that the trims are spaced evenly, begin by gluing on two roses, one at the top of the pillow and one at the bottom. Then glue the remaining roses and pearl flower trims evenly in between the first two roses.

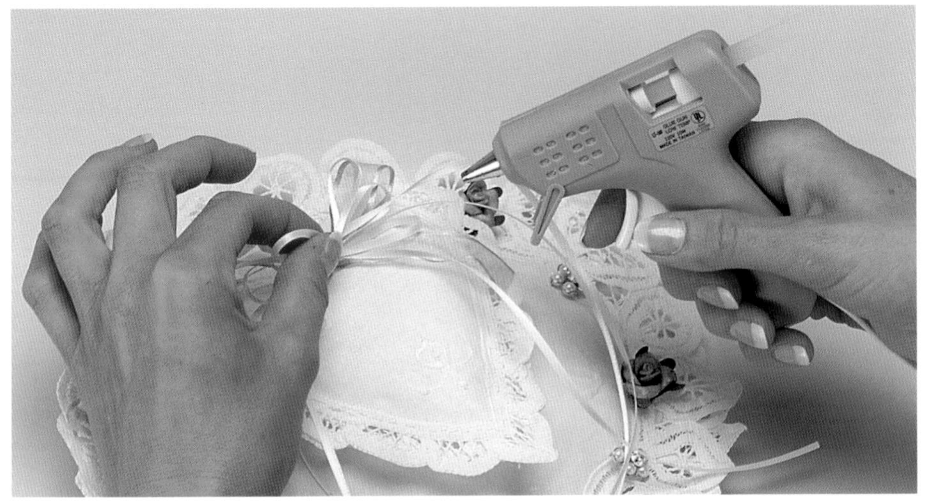

4 *Add Bows*
Tie a bow with a 15" (38cm) length of lavender ribbon and hot glue it onto the top center of the small heart pillow. Tie a bow with a 24" (61cm) piece of white ribbon and hot glue the bow onto the center of the lavender bow. Repeat with two more pieces of white ribbon, gluing each bow on top of the first white bow.

5 *Add Final Trims*
Hot glue the remaining three lavender roses in a cluster onto the center of the layered bows. Glue the remaining pearl flower trim just underneath the rose cluster.

Flower Fairy *Basket and Headpiece*

You'll capture the essence of a fairytale wedding with this enchanting rose petal basket and matching headpiece, perfect for your flower girl's jaunt down the aisle. Sprinkled with glistening fairy dust, these pieces are sure to add a touch of storybook magic to your wedding celebrations.

Materials List

- Delta Ceramcoat matte interior brush-on varnish
- iridescent crystal and ultra-fine glitter
- artificial pink and green berry sprigs
- pruning shears
- foam brush or flat paintbrush
- hot glue gun and glue sticks
- scissors
- ruler

Basket:

- small white grapevine or willow basket, approximately 8" to 9" (20cm to 23cm)
- 16 artificial roses: 15 pink and 1 yellow (with stems removed)
- three large green leaves, approximately 4 1/2" (11cm)
- artificial sprigs of cream baby's breath
- 5/8" (2cm) sheer pink wired ribbon
- 1 1/2" (4cm) sheer pink wired ribbon
- rose petals to fill basket

Headpiece:

- white satin headband
- ten green leaves, approximately 2" to 3" (5cm to 8cm)
- three 2 1/2" (6cm) artificial pink daisies (with stems removed)
- six 1 1/4" (3cm) white beaded pearl flower trims (with stems removed)
- 5/8" (16mm) sheer pink wired ribbon

Flower Fairy Basket

1. Use a foam brush or flat paintbrush to apply matte varnish to the leaves and basket. While still wet, sprinkle them with iridescent crystal and ultra-fine glitter. Allow them to dry. Hot glue the three glittered leaves into the inside center of the basket by the handle.

2. Hot glue the pink roses around the edge of the basket with the yellow rose in the center, just beneath the handle. Accent them with sprigs of berries and baby's breath.

3. Cut a 15" (38cm) length of the 5/8" (2cm) pink wired ribbon and a 24" (61cm) length of the 1 1/2" (4cm) pink ribbon. Wrap the 15" (38cm) piece of ribbon around the handle of the basket. Hot glue the ends to secure. Tie a bow with the 24" (61cm) piece of ribbon. Trim the ends to the desired length, then hot glue the bow onto the basket just under the yellow rose.

4. Fill the basket with rose petals.

Headpiece

1. Use a foam brush or a flat paintbrush to apply the matte varnish to the leaves. While they are still wet, sprinkle them with the iridescent crystal and ultra-fine glitter. Allow the leaves to dry. Hot glue the glittered leaves to cover the top surface of the headband.

2. Hot glue the three daisies onto the headband, with one in the center and one on each side. Hot glue the beaded flower trims and berry sprigs onto the headband.

3. Tie a bow with a 26" (66cm) length of the 5/8" (2cm) pink ribbon. Hot glue the bow onto the back of the headband at the top center. Entwine each length of the ribbon bow around the floral trims as desired. Hot glue to secure. Trim the ends of the ribbon to the desired length.

Unity *Candle and Tapers*

Découpaging ordinary pillar and taper candles with floral napkins is a quick and easy way to transform them into a unique, luminous centerpiece. As a finishing touch, the candles are embellished with miniature white doves, artificial floral trims and romantic pearl accents. These candles are so quick and easy to create that you may want to craft several more to decorate your reception tables.

❤ Materials List ❤

- 8" (20cm) ivory pillar candle
- two 10" (25cm) ivory taper candles
- Delta Ceramcoat satin découpage medium
- floral napkins
  Bridal Ribbons by Party Express
- iridescent crystal and ultra-fine glitter
- artificial cream roses and leaves: one large rose for the pillar candle and two smaller roses for the taper candles (with stems removed)
- artificial green berry sprigs, ferns and cream baby's breath sprigs
- four 1" (3cm) miniature white doves: two for the pillar candle and one for each taper candle
- 3mm white or ivory pearl string (for pillar candle only)
- candleholders
- hot glue gun and glue sticks
- foam brush or flat paintbrush
- scissors
- ruler

1. Tear the floral napkins into several pieces of various sizes. Apply the torn pieces of napkins onto the candles with the découpage medium, overlapping each piece as desired. (For visual interest and contrast, leave some areas of the candles exposed at the very top and bottom.) Apply additional coats of découpage medium over the surface of the napkins to seal them. While the final coat of découpage medium is still wet, sprinkle the surface with the iridescent crystal and ultra-fine glitter. Allow the candles to dry.
2. Apply the découpage medium onto the leaves. While they are still wet, sprinkle the leaves with the iridescent crystal and ultra-fine glitter. Allow the leaves to dry.
3. Hot glue the artificial ferns, glittered leaves, roses and berry sprigs onto the center of the candles. Accent the floral trims with the sprigs of artificial cream baby's breath.
4. Form two loops with 3 1/2" (9cm) pieces of pearl string. Hot glue the two pearl loops behind the top of the rose on the pillar candle.
5. Hot glue two miniature white doves onto the pillar candle and one on each of the taper candles.

Floral Découpage *Cornucopias*

Reminiscent of the romantic Victorian era, these floral cornucopias will add an elegant touch to your wedding ceremony décor. Using floral napkins and a simple découpage technique, you can transform ordinary paper cones into extraordinary keepsakes that will be treasured long after your wedding day has passed. Filled with tasty treats, these découpage cones would make charming favors for your wedding guests.

❤ Materials List ❤

- paper cones, 6¾" (17cm) long x 3" (8cm) in diameter
  ARTIFACTS ANGEL CONES
- floral napkins
  LAVENDER BOUQUET BY AMERICAN GREETING'S DESIGNWARE
- Delta Ceramcoat acrylic paint in Light Ivory
- Delta Ceramcoat satin découpage medium
- iridescent crystal and ultra-fine glitter
- artificial lavender hydrangea blooms with two 4" (10cm) leaves (with stems removed)
- three ¾" (2cm) miniature artificial cream roses with leaves (with stems removed)
- three ½" (1cm) miniature self-adhesive paper roses: two lavender and one cream
- sprigs of cream bridal lace
- 5/16" (8mm) sheer lavender ribbon
- 1¼" (3cm) lavender beaded pearl flower trim (with stem removed)
- two round lavender acrylic jewels
- pruning shears
- paintbrushes and general painting supplies
- hot glue gun and glue sticks
- scissors
- ruler

Dream Idea

Rose Petal Cones

Add a touch of pure romance to the traditional rose petal toss with these exquisite Victorian-style paper cones. Simply cut a large circle out of heavy printed scrapbook paper, then cut the circle into quarters or thirds, depending on the desired size. Use decorative-edge scissors along the top edge to cut a fancy border. Glue the paper into a cone shape and accent with a dainty paper doily. Add a ribbon hanger, bow and miniature paper roses. For the finishing touch, tuck a tulle circle inside the cone and add dried rose petals.

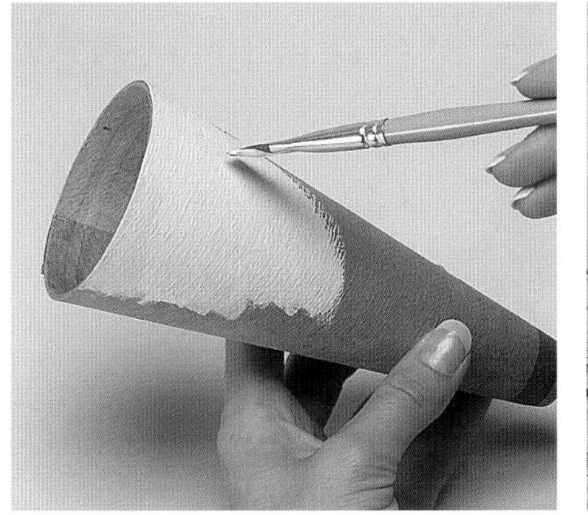

1 ***Basecoat Paper Cone***
Basecoat the paper cone with Light Ivory and allow it to dry.

2 ***Découpage Cone***
Tear the floral napkins into pieces of various sizes and shapes. Adhere the torn napkin pieces to the cone with découpage medium, overlapping the pieces as desired. For visual interest and contrast, leave some painted areas of the cone exposed.

Crafty Bride Tip

If using the cornucopia for a pew marker, adjust the hanger length accordingly.

3 ***Sprinkle Glitter onto Cone***
Apply additional coats of découpage medium over the surface of the napkins to seal them. While the final coat of découpage medium is still wet, sprinkle the surface with the iridescent crystal and ultra-fine glitter. Allow the cone to dry.

4 ***Fill Cone with Floral Trims***
Apply the découpage medium onto the leaves and sprinkle them with iridescent crystal and ultra-fine glitter while they are still wet. Allow them to dry. Hot glue the hydrangea blooms and the glittered leaves inside the cone, adhering the leaves at the back of the cone to allow the flowers to be completely visible. (Leave a little space free on both sides of the cone to glue the ribbon hanger in step 5.) Glue the three cream roses and the sprigs of cream baby's breath inside the cone to accent the hydrangea blooms.

5 ***Add Hanger and Final Trims***
Use a 15" (38cm) length of lavender ribbon to create a hanger for the cone by gluing the ends of the ribbon inside each side of the cone. Tie a bow with a 12" (30cm) length of lavender ribbon and hot glue it onto the top center of the cone. Hot glue the beaded flower trim onto the center of the bow. To finish, hot glue the miniature paper roses onto the cone, with the lavender roses at the top and bottom and the cream rose in the center. Glue the two lavender acrylic jewels in between the cream and lavender roses.

Blooming Heart *Wreath*

What could be more enchanting for a spring or garden wedding than this lovely floral heart wreath to welcome your special guests? Adorned with decorative moss, artificial blooms and romantic ribbon trims, this heart also makes a fresh alternative to the traditional pew bow. And best of all, because it is made with artificial flowers, the wreath can be displayed as a wedding keepsake in your home for years to come.

Materials List

- 12" (30cm) extruded foam heart wreath
- green sheet moss
- 1 1/2" (4cm) sheer pink ribbon
- artificial floral trims in pink, mauve, yellow and cream (roses, hydrangea blooms and sprigs of cream baby's breath with their stems removed)
- 1 1/4" (3cm) white beaded pearl flower trim (with stem removed)
- 3/8" (10mm) iridescent crystal pearl string
- floral spray adhesive (optional)
- pruning shears
- hot glue gun and glue sticks
- scissors
- ruler

1. Hot glue the sheet moss around the foam heart. (Or you could use floral spray adhesive to adhere the moss onto the heart form.)

2. Cut a 48" (122cm) length of the 1 1/2" (4cm) pink ribbon. Tie each end of the ribbon piece around the top sides of the heart to create a hanger. Trim the end pieces, then secure with hot glue.

3. Hot glue the floral trims onto the front of the foam heart. To ensure your heart wreath looks balanced, space the larger roses evenly around the wreath. Then, fill in the open spaces with the smaller roses and hydrangea blooms. The small clusters of baby's breath should be added at the end to fill in any gaps and to provide visual contrast to the larger flowers.

4. Tie a bow with a 22" (56cm) length of the 1 1/2" (4cm) sheer pink ribbon. Hot glue the bow onto the top center of the heart. Hot glue the white beaded flower trim onto the center of the bow.

5. Cut an 80" (203cm) length of the pearl string. Wrap the pearl string around the heart wreath, using hot glue to secure.

Mother's *Memory Corsage*

Your mother will no doubt shed a few tears of joy when you present this heartwarming memory corsage to her on your wedding day. Nestled on a delicate lace-trimmed handkerchief, the silk roses and feathery ferns are accented with a miniature charm containing a sentimental photo from the past. Your mother will delight in keeping her special memory of you close to her heart as you both celebrate the joy of your wedding day.

Materials List

- metal photo frame charm
  CHARMING THOUGHTS BY THE CARD CONNECTION
- small photo (or color copy) to fit inside frame
- green floral tape
- white or ivory lace-trimmed handkerchief
- stem of three artificial cream roses with leaves
- artificial fern spray
- 1" (3cm) pin clasp
- 1/4" (6mm) ivory ribbon
- small piece of green floral wire, approximately 3" (8cm)
- wire cutters
- hot glue gun and glue sticks
- scissors
- ruler

1. Cut the photo to fit inside the miniature frame. Place the photo inside.

2. Cut the stems of the roses and fern spray to the desired length, approximately 3" to 4" (8cm to 10cm), then wrap the stems together using the green floral tape. The fern should lie in the back of the roses as a subtle accent to the corsage.

3. Use floral tape to wrap the metal pin clasp to the back of the stem.

4. Cut a 24" (61cm) piece of the 1/4" (6mm) ivory ribbon. Beginning in the center, form four loops (two on each side), then twist a small piece of wire in the center to secure. Trim away the excess wire.

5. Cut a 12" (30cm) piece of the ivory ribbon. Insert one end of the ribbon piece into the metal loop of the photo charm, then securely tie the charm and the ivory ribbon loops around the stem of the corsage. Trim the ends of the ribbon to the desired length. Pin the corsage onto the handkerchief for the finishing touch. Present the corsage pinned to the handkerchief to the mother of the bride on the morning of the wedding. She can remove the corsage and pin it onto her dress, and she'll have a handkerchief close at hand in case tears of joy overwhelm her.

Forever in Our Hearts
Memory Bouquet

Your wedding is a joyful and often sentimental occasion, and throughout the day you'll most likely find yourself remembering those beloved friends and family members who are unable to be there. Pay tribute to the memory of lost loved ones and keep them close to your heart with this poignant floral centerpiece. You can display the bouquet in a place of honor during the ceremony, and bring it to the reception afterwards to keep loved ones close as you continue to celebrate your glorious day.

Materials List

Centerpiece:

- embossed ivory watering can, 5½" (14cm) tall
- floral foam brick
- green sheet moss
- 16-gauge gold wire (one piece of wire for each photo in the bouquet)
- assortment of photos (or color copies)
- artificial floral trims (an assortment of stemmed flowers in soft pastel shades of pink, yellow and cream; clusters of artificial ivy foliage; and green berries)
- three 6" x 24" (15cm x 61cm) pieces of white tulle
- ⅞" (2cm) sheer pink wired ribbon
- 1¼" (3cm) white beaded pearl flower trim (with stem removed)
- ⅜" (10mm) wooden dowel (to curl wire stems)
- needle-nose pliers
- transparent tape (optional)
- sharp knife
- wire cutters/pruning shears
- hot glue gun and glue sticks
- scissors
- ruler

"Forever in Our Hearts" Tag:

- pre-folded white place card
- heart sticker
- alphabet stickers

Crafty Bride Tip

After the ceremony, bring the memory bouquet to the reception to decorate a special table. You could also make several memory bouquets as your reception table centerpieces. Then, instead of assigning your guest tables with a number, you can continue the "memory" theme by naming each table after the beloved one whose photos are featured in that particular bouquet. The memory bouquets also make touching gifts to warm the hearts of special friends and family members.

1 *Arrange Bouquet*

Use a sharp knife to cut the floral foam brick to fit inside the watering can. Cut smaller pieces to fill in any open gaps. Hot glue the floral foam pieces to secure them inside the watering can. Add more hot glue between the seams of the brick pieces to stabilize them (see step 2 of Love in Full Bloom project, page 15). Hot glue the green sheet moss onto the foam base. Insert the stems of approximately 8 to 10 artificial flowers into the mossy foam base, placing them at different heights and tilting them at different angles to create a pleasing bouquet. Reserve some flowers to use as filler in step 3.

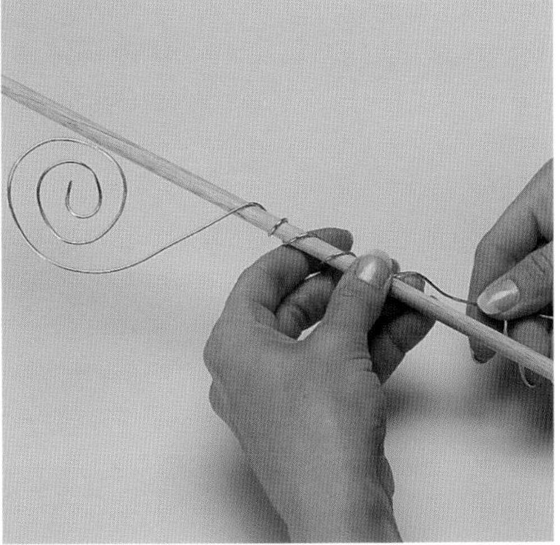

2 *Form Wire Photo Holders*

Use wire cutters to cut a 22" to 24" (56cm to 61cm) length of gold wire. Cut one wire piece for each photo in your bouquet and vary the lengths of the wire slightly for visual interest. Twist one end of a wire piece into a circular coiled shape into which the photo will be inserted. Hold one end of the wire with the needle-nose pliers and curl the wire into a spiral. Curl the remaining wire stem around a wooden dowel, leaving approximately 2 1/2" (6cm) of wire straight at the bottom to insert into the foam base. Repeat for each wire piece.

3 *Place Photo Holders, Add Floral Trims and Bows*

Insert the wire photo holders into the foam base in the watering can, interspersing them with the flowers. Cut the stems off of the remaining flowers and glue the buds, clusters of ivy foliage and berries onto the sheet moss, filling in empty areas around the stems of the flowers and the wire photo holders. Cut three pieces of 6" x 24" (15cm x 61cm) pieces of white tulle and tie each into a bow. Trim the ends of the bows to the desired length and fluff out the loops with your fingers. Glue the tulle bows into the floral bouquet.

4 *Add Final Trims to Watering Can*

Tie a bow with a 20" (51cm) length of pink wired ribbon and hot glue it onto the front center rim of the watering can. Hot glue the beaded flower trim onto the center of the bow.

5 *Arrange Photos in Bouquet*

To finish, insert the photos into the wire holders. If necessary, secure the backs of the photos with transparent tape. If desired, add a "Forever in Our Hearts" tag or personalize the bouquet with the names of the loved ones featured in the photos.

LOVE
makes a garden grow!
Nicole and Steve • June 12, 2004
WITH LOVE

Sweet Sentiments

The tradition of giving wedding favors dates back to a bygone era when, according to superstitious folklore, receiving a token of thanks from the bride and groom was considered good luck. Today the favors given to wedding guests are regarded as thoughtful keepsakes that serve as lasting reminders of your special day.

Your gifts and favors do not have to be elaborate or expensive to make a "favorable" impression. In this chapter, you'll discover that with just a touch of imagination and creativity, you can craft the simplest of trims into delightful take-home wedding keepsakes.

First and foremost, you'll want your favors to tie in with your wedding theme and to reflect your own personal style. Brides who are sweet on tradition will love the fresh look of the festive favor boxes and romantic sachet bags (page 41) using contemporary scrapbook trims and embellishments.

The fun and functional wine charms and beaded plant poke favors (pages 46 and 42) are sure to make a lasting impression on your guests. They'll look great decorating the tables at the reception, and the guests will also love putting them to good use at home.

If you're short on table space or desire a less cluttered look at your reception, the perfect solution is to design favors that also serve as place cards for your guests. The miniature rose pots and watering can favors (pages 38 and 40) do just that with their decorative wire stems, which are perfect for tucking in your guests' name cards.

Regardless of your wedding style, you're sure to wow your guests with any one of these fanciful favor and gift ideas.

Rose

Inspired by the romantic charm of an English rose garden, these delicate potted blooms are place cards as well as wedding favors. A medley of miniature terra cotta pots is painted in subtle pastel hues and antiqued with soft strokes of metallic gold. Artificial rose blossoms are then planted in the pots, which are adorned with charming button and bow accents. Decorative wire stems hold the name cards, and can later be used to display a favorite photo.

Crafty Bride Tip

I painted the pots in a rainbow of soft pastel shades, but you could use one color that matches your wedding theme. You can also consider making larger versions of these rose pots for the center of each reception table to hold menus, table numbers or a printed program of the evening's festivities.

Materials List

- $2\frac{1}{4}$" (6cm) clay pots
- Delta Ceramcoat acrylic paints in Ivory, Hydrangea Pink, Village Green and Metallic Kim Gold
- Delta Ceramcoat matte interior spray varnish
- floral foam bricks
- green sheet moss
- artificial ivory roses with leaves (with stems removed)
- artificial sprigs of cream baby's breath
- $\frac{5}{8}$" (2cm) gold-accented sheer ribbon
- $\frac{1}{8}$" (3mm) ivory ribbon
- 16-gauge gold wire
- ivory flower-shaped buttons
- place cards (Use pre-folded white place cards, alphabet stickers and miniature flower stickers.)
- needle-nose pliers
- sharp knife
- old toothbrush (for spattering)
- paintbrushes and general painting supplies
- wire cutters
- paper towels
- hot glue gun and glue sticks
- scissors
- ruler

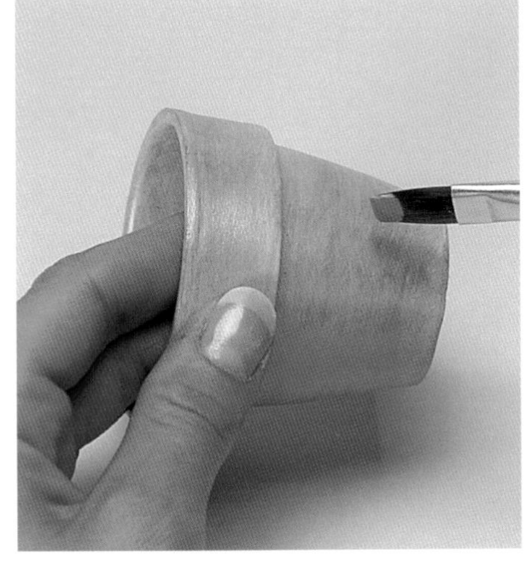

1 *Apply Gold Wash to Pots*

Basecoat the pots in your desired colors, such as Ivory, Hydrangea Pink and Village Green. When the pots are dry, antique them with a wash of Metallic Kim Gold. Mix a few drops of water with a dab of gold paint and apply it onto the pot with a paintbrush. Wipe away any excess gold paint with a paper towel. Add extra coats as necessary to achieve the desired shade.

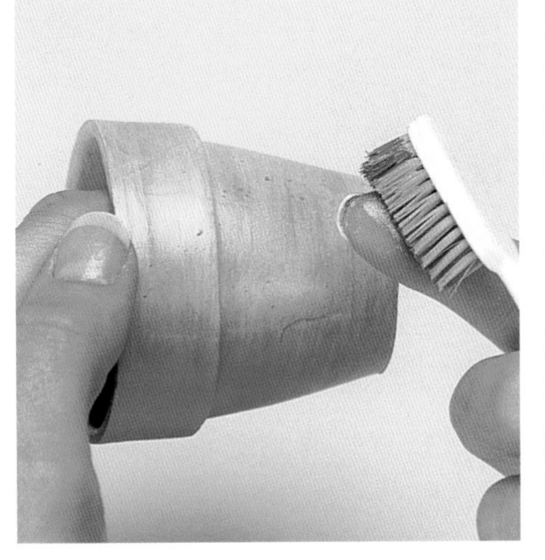

2 *Spatter Pots with Gold Paint*

Use an old, worn toothbrush to spatter the pots with Metallic Kim Gold (see Terms & Techniques, page 10). When the pots are dry, apply the matte spray varnish.

3 *Glue Roses into Pots*

Using a sharp knife, cut the floral foam bricks into small pieces that fit inside the clay pots. Hot glue the foam pieces inside the pots to secure them. Hot glue the green sheet moss over the foam, covering it completely. Hot glue an artificial rose and leaves onto the mossy base of each pot. Hot glue sprigs of artificial baby's breath to accent the roses.

4 *Form Wire Place Card Holders*

Cut a 12" (30cm) length of gold wire using wire cutters. Twist one end of the wire piece into a circular coiled shape in which to place the name card. To twist the wire, hold one end of the wire with the needle-nose pliers and curl the wire into a spiral shape. Repeat for each pot.

5 *Add Final Trims and Insert Place Cards*

Cut a 12" (30cm) length of 5/8" (2cm) gold-accented sheer ribbon and tie it into a bow. Trim the ends of the bow to the desired length and hot glue it onto the front of the pot. Tie a 9" (23cm) length of 1/8" (3mm) ivory ribbon into a bow and trim the ends to the desired length. Hot glue the ivory bow onto the center of the larger gold bow. Hot glue the flower-shaped button onto the center of the bows. Repeat for each pot. Use alphabet stickers to personalize each place card and add floral stickers as accents. Insert the place cards into the coiled wire shapes, and insert the wire stems into the floral foam.

Mini Watering Can *Place Cards*

For a fresh-from-the-garden favor idea, these miniature, vintage-style watering cans make charming place card holders. Decorated with moss, artificial blooms and other romantic trims, these stylish accents are sure to add a touch of garden whimsy to your wedding celebrations. As a fun variation to a place card holder, you can use the coiled wire stem to display a favorite photo or to tuck in a colorful flower seed packet as a favor.

Amy

Carol

Materials List

- 3" (8cm) miniature embossed ivory watering cans
- floral foam bricks
- green sheet moss
- 16-gauge gold wire
- artificial floral trims: 1 1/2" (4cm) pink and/or lavender paper roses; 3/4" (2cm) yellow paper roses; 1/2" (1cm) miniature self-adhesive paper roses in pink, lavender and yellow; and small leaves
- 5/16" (8mm) sheer pink, lavender and yellow ribbon
- 3/4" (2cm) pearl flower trims (with stems removed)
- 4mm crystal iridescent pearl string
- pre-folded white place cards
- alphabet and heart stickers
- sharp knife
- 3/8" (10mm) wooden dowel (to curl wire stems)
- wire cutters
- needle-nose pliers
- hot glue gun and glue sticks
- scissors
- ruler

1. Using a sharp knife, cut the floral foam bricks into small pieces to fit inside the watering cans. Hot glue the foam pieces inside the cans to secure them.

2. Hot glue the green sheet moss onto the foam base.

3. Hot glue the floral trims as desired onto the front of the watering can and around the mossy base. In the center of each base, glue a 4" (10cm) looped piece of the pearl string and a miniature paper rose.

4. Cut pieces of gold wire approximately 18" (46cm) in length. You will need one piece of wire for each watering can favor. Twist one end of the wire piece into a circular coiled shape in which to place your name card. To twist the wire, hold one end of the wire with the needle-nose pliers and curl the wire into a spiral shape (see step 4 in the Rose Place Card Pots project, page 39). Curl the remaining wire stem around the wooden dowel, leaving approximately 2 1/2" (6cm) of wire straight at the bottom. Insert the straight end of the wire stems into the floral foam bases.

5. Tie the 14" (36cm) lengths of ribbon into bows at the top of the wire stems. Trim the ends of the bows to the desired length. Hot glue the pearl flower trims onto the centers of the bows.

6. To make your decorated place cards, use pre-folded white place cards packaged in bulk. Use alphabet stickers to personalize each card, and then add a heart sticker onto either side. Hot glue a miniature self-adhesive paper rose onto the top center of each heart sticker. Insert the place cards into the circular coiled shapes at the top of each wire stem.

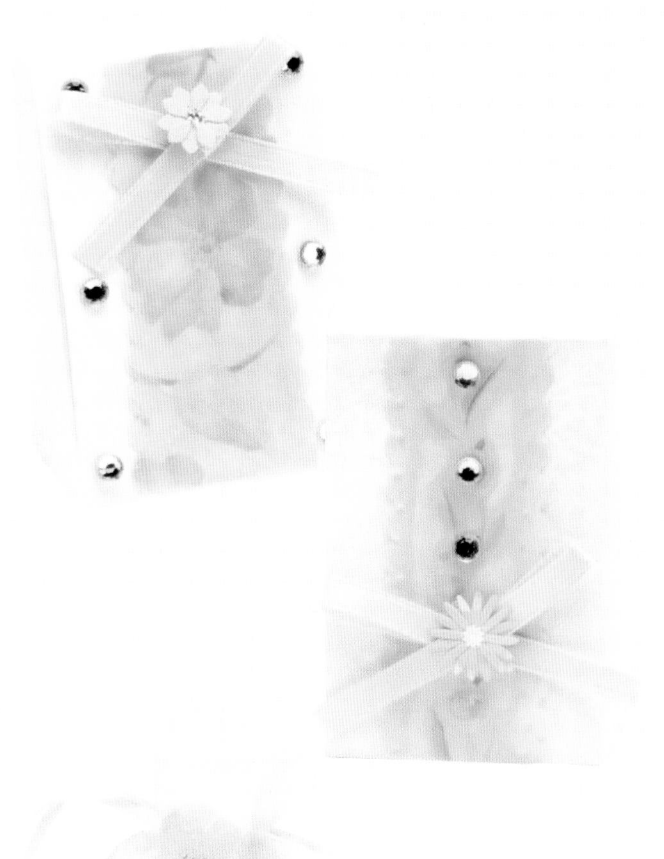

Scrappy Sweets *Favors*

Add a fresh and contemporary look to traditional favor boxes and sachet bags using a variety of scrapbook trims and embellishments. You can use the paper accents to coordinate other elements of your wedding, such as invitations, programs, place cards and even your wedding décor. Check out the Love Nest Birdhouse (page 64) to see how you can use scrapbook accents as quick and easy decorative trims.

❤ Materials List ❤

Favor Boxes:

- cream embossed favor boxes, 2" x 3" (5cm x 8cm)
- embossed vellum scrapbook papers
- vellum tape or double-sided tape
- assorted ribbon trims
- scrapbook paper embellishments
- round acrylic jewels
- sweets of your choice
- decorative-edge scissors
- hot glue gun and glue sticks
- scissors
- ruler

Sachet Bags:

- 3" (8cm) ivory drawstring sachet bags
- scrapbook paper embellishments
- sweets of your choice
- hot glue gun and glue sticks

Favor Boxes:

1. Cut strips of vellum scrapbook paper approximately 1 1/2" x 3" (4cm x 8cm). Trim the 3" (8cm) length of each side using decorative-edge scissors. Attach the pieces of scrapbook paper onto the center of each favor box using vellum tape or double-sided tape.

2. Hot glue bows, acrylic jewels and paper flower embellishments onto each box as desired. Or you can glue a piece of ribbon around the box, then accent the box with a variety of scrapbook trims and embellishments. Note: Be sure to fill the box with the sweets of your choice before gluing ribbon around any openings.

Sachet Bags:

1. Slip a small piece of cardboard inside the bags so that the hot glue does not run through the fabric. Accent the bags by hot gluing a variety of scrapbook trims and embellishments onto the front of each bag.

2. Fill the bags with the sweets of your choice, then tie the top of each bag closed.

Jeweled Heart

Fashioned from wire and beads, these fanciful plant poke favors will steal the hearts of your wedding day guests. For a personalized touch, add a printed tag to the wire stem of each favor accented with an acrylic heart jewel and an elegant bow trim. For a touch of garden whimsy, insert your plant poke favors into your floral centerpieces or into individually potted plants placed at each table setting.

Materials List

- 16-gauge gold wire
- 24-gauge gold wire
- assorted beads (approximately 38 to 40 for each plant poke, but amount varies depending on the size of the beads)
- thin liner paintbrush (use handle to wrap wire accent)
- needle-nose pliers
- wire cutters
- ruler

Tags:

- white cardstock
- heart-shaped acrylic jewels
- 1/8" (3mm) gold wired ribbon
- decorative-edge scissors
- 1/8" (3mm) hole punch
- hot glue gun and glue sticks
- computer and printer

Crafty Bride Tip

Use a 3" (8cm) heart-shaped cookie cutter to shape the wire heart. Simply wrap the wire around the outside of the heart shape with your fingers.

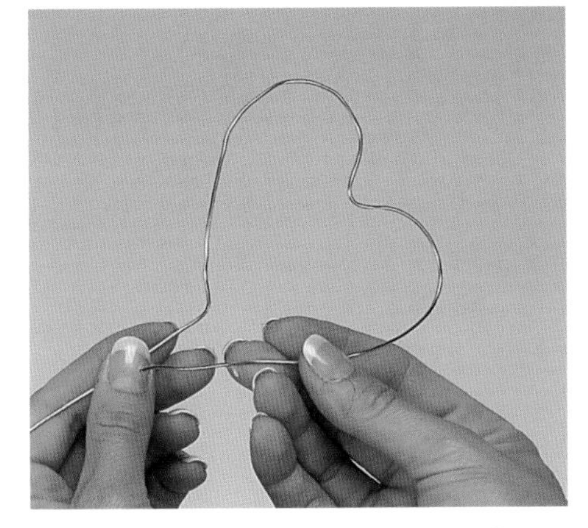

1 ***Cut Wire and Form Heart Shape***
Cut a 20" (51cm) piece of the heavy 16-gauge gold wire using wire cutters. Measure approximately 8" (20cm) from the bottom of the wire stem and bend the remaining 12" (30cm) of wire into a heart shape.

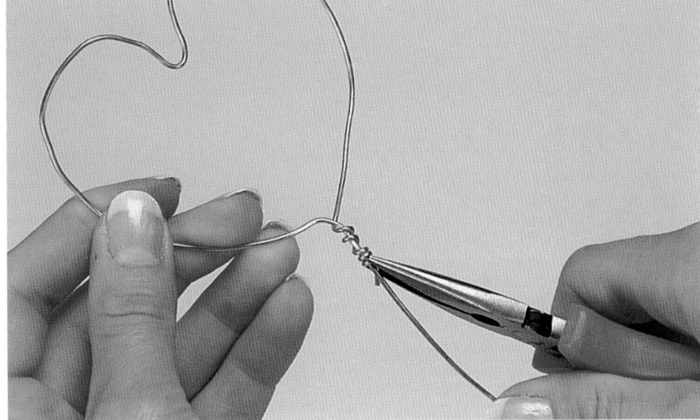

2 ***Wrap Wire Around Base of Heart to Secure***
Use needle-nose pliers to wrap the end of the wire used to make the heart around the long stem end of the wire several times. Continue to wrap the wire until it is secure. Use your fingers to further define the heart into the desired shape.

3 ***String Beads onto Wire and Wrap Around Heart***
Cut a 32" (81cm) length of the thin 24-gauge gold wire. Wrap one end of the wire piece five or six times around the bottom of the wire heart shape to secure it. String a few beads (three or five usually works best) onto the wire and then wrap it around the wire heart several times to secure. Continue to add beads and wrap the wire until the entire heart shape is beaded. Trim away any excess wire using the wire cutters.

4 ***Create Curlicue Embellishment***
Cut a 9" (23cm) length of the 24-gauge gold wire. Twist the center around the stem at the base of the heart until it's secure (so you have equal lengths of wire on each side). String a few beads (again, three or five beads work well) on one side and twist the remaining wire into a tight coil by wrapping it around the handle of a thin liner brush to form a decorative curlicue shape. Repeat on the other side.

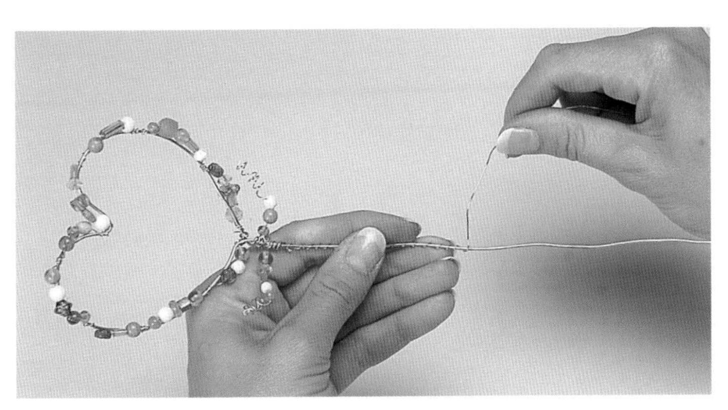

5 ***Wrap Wire Around Stem***
Cut an 18" (46cm) piece of the 24-gauge wire (length varies slightly depending on how closely you wrap the wire). Begin at the top of the stem (the base of the heart shape) and wrap the wire piece tightly around the entire length of the stem, ending at the very bottom. If necessary, trim any excess wire with the wire cutters. Secure the end around the bottom of the stem with pliers. If desired, add personalized tags that read "LOVE...makes a garden grow!" Cut tags with decorative-edge scissors and embellish them with heart-shaped jewels and gold bows. Punch a hole in one corner of each tag and tie them to the wire hearts with the gold ribbon.

Petal *Envelope Favors*

Use your own unique wedding theme as inspiration to transform plain petal envelopes into charming wedding favors. Romantic scrapbook papers provide the perfect backdrop to decorate with your favorite trims and embellishments. The envelope is the perfect size and shape to hold a CD of music or photos. Or tuck a different favor inside, perhaps a sentimental poem or a packet of flower seeds.

Materials List

- petal envelopes (Use ready-made or make your own from quality cardstock [see template, page 77].)
- scrapbook papers
- desired trims and embellishments
- favors to insert into your decorated petal envelopes
- glue pen or double-sided tape
- decorative-edge scissors
- hot glue gun and glue sticks
- pencil
- scissors

Crafty Bride Tip

You can use just about anything to decorate your petal envelopes. Browse the aisles of your favorite craft store and pick up scrapbook stickers, borders and photo corners, three-dimensional craft trims for scrapbooking and card making, ribbons, acrylic jewels, pearl strings, artificial floral trims and miniature garden accessories.

1. To save time, purchase your petal envelopes pre-packaged at your local specialty paper store. If you choose to make your own envelopes, simply trace and cut out the pattern on page 77 using quality cardstock paper..

2. If making your own envelopes, firmly slide the pointed edge of the bone folder along the edge of a ruler along each of the four sides (see dotted lines on template, page 77), then fold each petal flap inward until fully closed. (Note: Scoring the paper before folding it makes it easier to fold, especially when working with heavier-weight paper or cardstock.) To create a crisp crease on each fold, use the rounded end of the bone folder and gently move it up and down along the fold (see Terms & Techniques, page 11).

3. With the four petal flaps folded in, trace around the envelope onto the desired piece of scrapbook paper. Cut out the piece of scrapbook paper, then trim around the edges with the decorative-edge scissors.

4. Attach the scrapbook paper onto the front of the envelope using a glue pen or double-sided tape.

5. Embellish the envelope as desired. (Note: Remember to tuck the desired favor inside the envelope before you wrap it with scrapbook border stickers or glue ribbon pieces around the envelope.)

Photo Keepsake

Your thank-you cards become instant keepsakes when graced with a special wedding photo. Simply use blank cardstock as the base for the card and accent the photo of your choice with scrapbook papers, miniature paper roses, silver heart charms and romantic ribbon trims. Perfect for hanging, these keepsake cards will surely warm the hearts and homes of your family and friends for years to come.

Materials List

- large folded note cards, 5 1/8" x 7 3/8" (13cm x 19cm)
- embossed scrapbook paper
  K&Company's Juliana Printed Embossed Paper
- wedding photos or color copies (a smaller size such as 3 1/2" x 5" [9cm x 13cm] works best)
- 5/16" (8mm) sheer lavender ribbon
- 1/8" (3mm) silver metallic ribbon to frame outside edges of photo
- 1/2" (1cm) silver heart button or charm
- four 1/2" (1cm) miniature self-adhesive pink paper roses
- "With Love" printed white and silver ribbon (optional)
- decorative-edge scissors
- double-sided tape
- hot glue gun and glue sticks
- pencil
- scissors
- ruler

1. Using one of the note cards as a template, trace around the folded card onto a piece of embossed scrapbook paper. Cut out the scrapbook paper, then trim around the edges with the decorative-edge scissors.
2. Using double-sided tape, adhere the piece of scrapbook paper onto the center of the card. Press firmly until secure.
3. Cut a 9" (23cm) length of the 5/16" (8mm) sheer lavender ribbon. Form a loop, then hot glue the ends of the loop onto the top center of the back of the photo to create a hanger. Use the double-sided tape to attach the photo (with the ribbon hanger) onto the center of the card.
4. Measure the length and width of your photo. Then, cut four pieces of the 1/8" (3mm) silver metallic ribbon, one for the top and bottom and one for each side. Hot glue the ribbon pieces around the edges of the photo.
5. Tie a 12" (30cm) length of the sheer lavender ribbon into a bow. Trim the ends of the bow to the desired length. Hot glue the bow onto the card at the bottom of the ribbon hanger. Hot glue a silver heart charm or button onto the center of the bow.
6. Hot glue four miniature pink paper roses, one in each corner of the photo, to hide the seams of the ribbon trim.
7. If desired, adhere a piece of the "With Love" printed ribbon onto the bottom of the card.

Charming *Wine Favors*

Add a stylish touch to your wedding-day celebrations with these charming wine-themed party favors. They're a cinch to make using store-bought wine charm accessories and an assortment of scrapbook papers and embellishments. For a whimsical touch, add an actual wine cork accented with colorful beads and ribbon trims.

Materials List

- textured cream cardstock, $5\frac{1}{2}$" (14cm) squares (Make them yourself or purchase in bulk packages at a specialty paper store.)
- floral printed vellum scrapbook paper
  PANSY BY IT TAKES TWO
- beverage I.D. hoops
- assortment of wine-themed charms, beads and metal spacers
- 20-gauge silver wire
- wine corks
- $\frac{5}{16}$" (8mm) sheer ribbon in pink and lavender
- $\frac{1}{2}$" (1cm) miniature self-adhesive pink and cream paper roses
- wine bottle and glass stickers
  WINE COLLECTION BY STICKOPOTAMUS
- "With Love" white and silver metallic printed ribbon (optional)
- vellum tape or double-sided tape
- decorative-edge scissors
- $\frac{1}{16}$" (2mm) circle punch, or standard $\frac{1}{8}$" (3mm) hole punch
- drill with smal drill bit ($\frac{1}{16}$" [2mm])
- wire cutters
- needle-nose pliers
- thin liner paintbrush (use handle to wrap wire)
- hot glue gun and glue sticks
- pencil
- scissors
- ruler

Crafty Bride Tip

Certain brands of glue may cause the vellum paper to bubble. It's best to use vellum tape or double-sided tape when adhering the vellum paper onto cardstock.

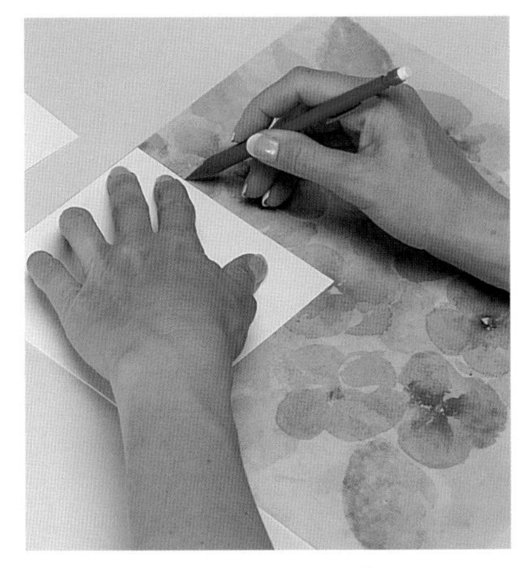

1 ***Trace Square onto Vellum Paper***
Using a $5\frac{1}{2}$" (14cm) square of textured cream cardstock as a template, trace a square onto a piece of floral vellum scrapbook paper.

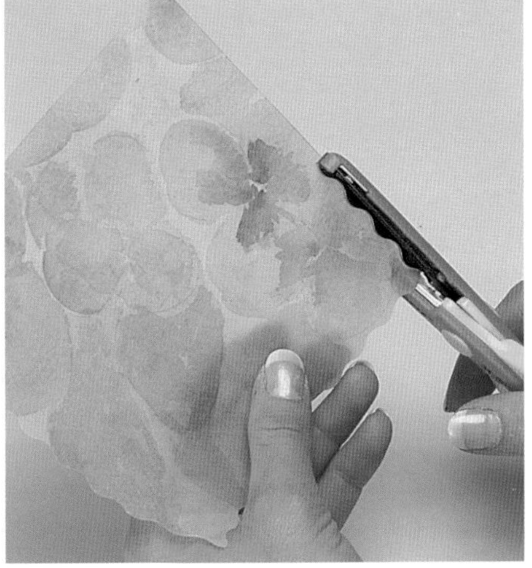

2 ***Create Decorative Edge***
Cut out the square with scissors and then trim around the edges with the decorative-edge scissors.

3 ***Attach Vellum to Cardstock***
Attach the vellum square onto the center of a $5\frac{1}{2}$" (14cm) cardstock square using the vellum or double-sided tape.

4 ***Assemble Wine Charms***
Assemble the wine charms by stringing one metal spacer, three beads, a charm in the middle, and then three beads and one spacer on the other side of the charm onto the beverage I.D. hoops.

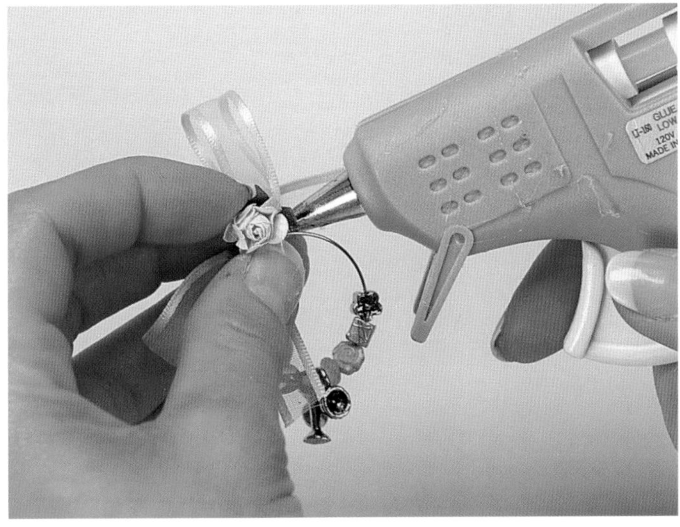

5 ***Add Bows***
Tie a 10" (25cm) length of the $\frac{5}{16}$" (8mm) ribbon into a bow around the top of the metal hoop and trim the ends of the bow to the desired length. Hot glue a miniature paper rose onto the center of each bow.

Crafty Bride Tip

To add a personalized touch to your wine charm favors, you can order custom-printed ribbon with your names and wedding date, then attach a piece of this ribbon to the wine cork in place of the "With Love" printed ribbon.

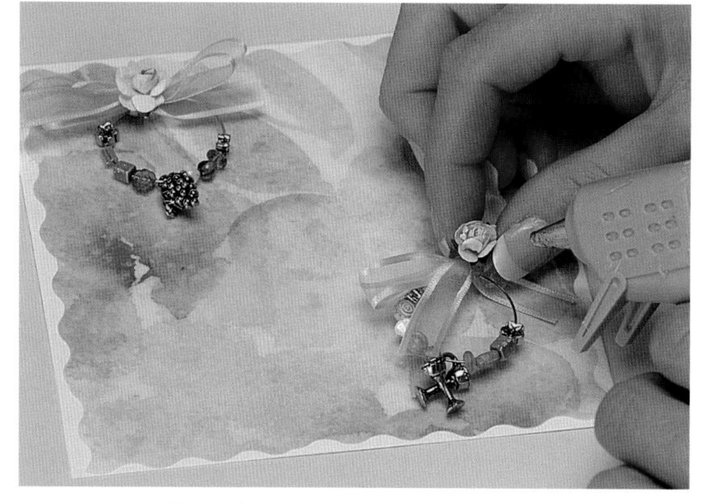

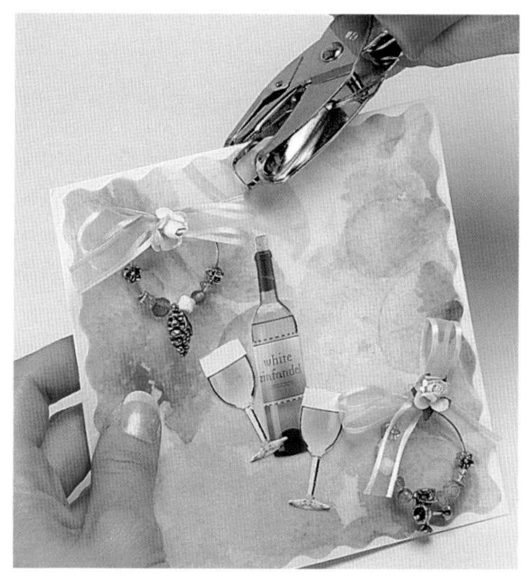

6 *Attach Wine Charms to Card*
To attach the wine charms onto each card, place a dab of hot glue behind the ribbon bow on each hoop, then press it onto the card until secure. You can vary your designs by placing the wine charms in the top left and right corners or in a diagonal position in opposite corners. If desired, use four charms on each card, gluing one in each corner.

7 *Add Stickers and Punch Hole*
Add the wine-themed stickers to the card as desired. Punch a hole in the top center of the card using the 1/16" (2mm) circle punch or 1/8" (3mm) hole punch.

8 *Twist Wire into Hole*
Using wire cutters, cut a 9" (23cm) piece of silver wire. Insert one end of the wire piece into the hole at the top of the card and twist the end around the stem end of the wire to secure it. Use needle-nose pliers to secure the very end of the wire.

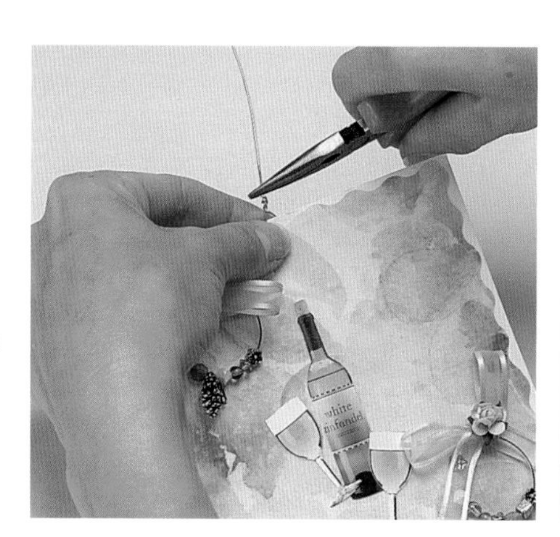

9 *Drill Hole in Wine Cork*
Drill a tiny hole through the center of the wine cork using the small drill bit (1/16" [2mm]).

10 *Add Cork and Final Trims*
If desired, accent the cork by gluing on a piece of "With Love" ribbon. Insert the wire piece through the hole in the cork. Add five beads, then tightly curl the remaining wire around the handle of a small liner paintbrush. Trim any excess wire with the wire cutters.

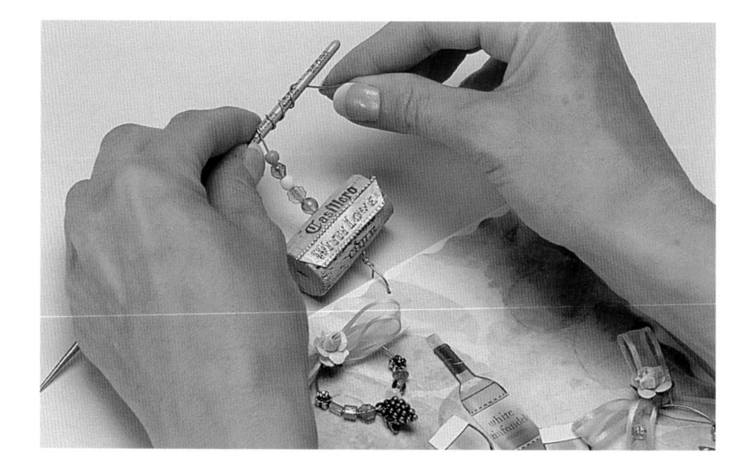

Flower Girl *Teddy Bear*

Dress a cuddly teddy bear as a miniature version of your flower girl for the perfect gift idea! Our furry friend wears a romantic floral headpiece and carries a miniature basket of blooms accented with a personalized gift tag. For a heartwarming touch, include a favorite photo of your flower girl and you in a decorated magnetic photo frame.

Materials List

- 14" (36cm) plush teddy bear
- small white basket, approximately 2 1/2" to 3" (6cm to 8cm) square
- 4" (10cm) white crocheted doily
- 6" (15cm) piece of a mini dusty rose floral garland and matching floral trims
- 1 1/2" (4cm) pink floral satin ribbon
- 1/2" (1cm) ivory braided trim to glue around edge of basket
- four 3/4" (2cm) miniature pink paper roses
- four miniature pink silk flower clusters
- 5/16" (8mm) pink sheer ribbon
- 1/2" (1cm) miniature self-adhesive pink paper roses
- 3/8" (9mm) pearl string
- personalized gift tag
- photo of your flower girl and you in a clear acrylic frame (optional)
- hot glue gun and glue sticks
- scissors
- ruler

1. Cut a 6" (15cm) piece of the mini floral garland, then hot glue it onto the top of the bear's head for the headpiece. Accent the floral headpiece with three of the 3/4" (2cm) pink paper roses and three of the pink flower clusters.

2. Drape one of the 13 1/2" (34cm) pieces of the pearl string along the length of the floral headpiece. Hot glue it to secure.

3. Cut the doily in half, then hot glue one of the doily halves onto the neck area of the bear to create the lace collar.

4. Tie a 22" (56cm) length of the 1 1/2" (4cm) ribbon into a bow. Trim the ends of the bow to the desired length. Hot glue the bow onto the center of the doily collar. Hot glue the remaining 3/4" (2cm) pink rose onto the center of the bow.

5. Hot glue the remaining piece of pearl string around the bear's neck to make a necklace.

6. Hot glue a piece of ivory braided trim around the edge of the basket. Glue floral trims inside the basket, and then accent the center with the remaining pink flower cluster. Tie a 10" (25cm) length of the 5/16" (8mm) sheer pink ribbon into a bow. Trim the ends of the bow to the desired length. Hot glue the bow onto the basket, then hot glue a miniature pink paper rose onto the center of the bow. Hot glue the basket onto the teddy bear's arm. Add a personalized tag to the basket with curling ribbon. If desired, include a photo in a clear acrylic frame decorated with romantic trims and alphabet beads that spell out your flower girl's name.

6
Wedding
Wedding
Wedding
LOVE
Wishes

Let's Celebrate!

Your wedding reception is the perfect opportunity to express your creative style and to give your family and friends a party they'll never forget! And luckily, your reception does not have to be elaborate or expensive to make a lasting impression. In this chapter, you'll learn how to create simple handmade touches that will set your event apart from all the rest.

You'll discover how to create a heart garland with twinkling fairy lights (page 60) and floral candle lanterns (page 55) that light up the night and create a romantic ambience. In addition, you'll learn how to give a vintage bird cage a contemporary look as a card holder with sparkling butterfly accents and a lovely bouquet of artificial blooms (page 54).

Of course, no wedding reception is ever complete without a cake, and your confection will look lovely adorned by the Floral Heart Cake Topper (page 56). Add a charming touch to each table with miniature guest books (page 52) that will give your wedding guests the opportunity to become more creative with their wedding wishes. For those of you brides who love sweet surprises, give your guests an unexpected pleasure with the Tasty Treat Table Numbers (page 62) and candy-inspired centerpieces (page 65). For an extra sweet touch, accent the candy centerpieces with favorite childhood photos of you and your groom.

Whether you're dreaming of twinkling lights, heavenly hearts or tasty childhood sweets, these fresh and fun ideas are guaranteed to make your celebration more memorable than you ever imagined.

Wedding Wishes *Guest Books*

Put a modern twist on the traditional guest book by scattering these handcrafted miniature versions on your reception tables. Fashioned from sheets of textured watercolor paper, these accordion-style guest books are blank inside to present a fresh and creative alternative to the simple signature. As a fun variation, you can use the scrapbook frames to personalize the guest books with a favorite photo. Or to liven things up a bit, place instant cameras on each table for your guests to add their own goofy photos!

Materials List

- artist's size pieces of textured ivory paper
  STRATHMORE
- assorted scrapbook papers
  ROMANTIC PAPERS FROM THE ANNA GRIFFIN COLLECTION WORK WELL
- alphabet stickers
- $^{5}/_{16}$" (8mm) sheer ribbon in pink, ivory or lavender
- $2^{1}/_{4}$" (5cm) square scrapbooking frames
  MAKING MEMORIES CHARMED FRAMES
- silver 6mm cube alphabet beads (to spell "love")
- $^{3}/_{4}$" (2cm) miniature artificial roses in pink, cream and lavender (with stems removed)
- double-sided tape
- decorative-edge scissors
- bone folder
- hot glue gun and glue sticks
- pencil
- scissors
- ruler

Dream Idea

Bride's Brag Book

As a fun alternative to the guest books, you can use this same crafting technique to create miniature keepsake photo albums. Follow steps 1 and 2 to create your miniature album. Then just add your favorite photos and use floral or wedding-themed scrapbook frames and stickers to decorate the pages. These miniature brag books make wonderful thank-you gifts for your parents and wedding party attendants.

Crafty Bride Tip

Scoring paper makes it easier to fold, especially when working with heavier-weight paper and cardstock. If you don't have a bone folder, a dull butter knife also works well to score and smooth the folds.

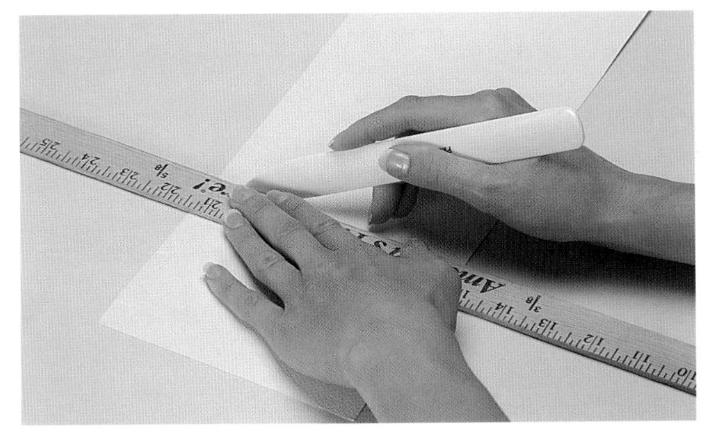

1 Measure and Score Paper

Cut a piece of textured ivory paper to 6" x 25" (15cm x 64cm). Along the 25" (64cm) length of the paper, add small pencil marks at the top and bottom of the paper at 5" (13cm) intervals. Align the ruler on the 5" (13cm) mark and slide the pointed end of the bone folder along the ruler's edge to score a fold line. Continue to score the paper at each 5" (13cm) interval. After scoring the fold lines, erase the pencil marks.

2 Fold Paper Accordion-Style

Once the paper has been scored, fold it accordion-style. After making each fold, gently move the rounded end of the bone folder up and down along the fold to create a crisp crease.

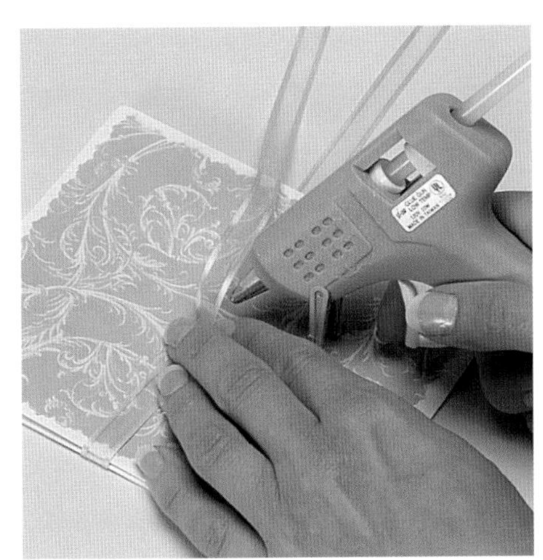

3 Cut Out Paper Squares

Trace a 5" x 6" (13cm x 15cm) rectangular shape onto the scrapbook paper (you can use the folded ivory paper as a template) and cut it out with scissors. Cut around the edges of the rectangle using decorative-edge scissors. Repeat for each book, using different kinds of scrapbook paper for each cover, if desired.

4 Adhere Paper to Book and Secure Ribbon

Using double-sided tape, adhere the scrapbook paper to the front center of the book's cover. Fold a 24" (61cm) piece of ribbon in half. Position the center point of the ribbon along the left edge of the book to ensure that there will be equal amounts of ribbon along the front and back of the book. Wrap the ribbon around the center of the book and secure it in the front center with a small dab of hot glue. (Do not glue the ribbon onto the back or you will be unable to open the accordion fold.) Tie a bow at the right side to keep the folds of the book closed. Trim the ends of the bow to the desired length.

5 Add Final Trims and Stickers

Cut a piece of textured ivory paper to fit behind the opening of the small square scrapbooking frame, and hot glue the frame onto the paper to secure it. Hot glue the frame with the paper onto the center of the book. Glue a miniature artificial rose inside the top of the frame and glue the "Love" alphabet cubes directly below it. Spell out "Wedding" above the frame and "Wishes" below it with the alphabet stickers. Repeat steps 1 through 5 for each book.

Bird Cage *Card Holder*

A newly purchased vintage-style bird cage becomes an exquisite card holder when decorated with sparkling butterfly accents and a romantic floral bouquet. As a unique twist, the bouquet is removable and can be used during your reception as a charming throw-away bouquet. After your wedding, the bird cage makes a lovely addition to your bed or bath décor.

Materials List

- white or ivory distressed bird cage, 12" wide x 8¼" deep x 19½" high (30cm x 21cm x 50cm)
- three 5" (13cm) jumbo butterfly accents in soft, pastel shades of pink, green and yellow
- twelve artificial rose stems in shades of soft pink and yellow
- clusters of artificial baby's breath
- 1½" (4cm) ivory satin ribbon
- ¼" (6mm) pink and ivory gold-beaded craft trim
- floral wire
- green floral tape
- wire cutters or pruning shears
- hot glue gun and glue sticks
- scissors
- ruler

1. Use the green floral tape to wrap the stems of the artificial roses into a bouquet. You will want to position the flowers at various heights to create fullness to the bouquet. If necessary, you can use wire cutters or pruning shears to cut any excess wire off of the stems so they are even at the bottom.
2. Cut a 30" (76cm) length of the 1½" (4cm) ivory satin ribbon, then wrap the ribbon piece tightly around the stems. Hot glue to secure.
3. Cut a 15" (38cm) length of the ¼" (6mm) beaded craft trim. Hot glue one end of the trim at the top of the handle, just underneath the floral bouquet. Then, wrap the trim several times around the ribbon handle (spaced evenly) until you have reached the very bottom. Hot glue the bottom end to secure.
4. Hot glue clusters of artificial baby's breath into the bouquet of roses.
5. Using a piece of floral wire, attach the bouquet to the center of the bird cage.
6. Use pieces of floral wire to attach the three butterflies to the cage as desired.

Floral Gel *Candle Lantern*

Add a touch of garden whimsy to your wedding celebration with this twinkling floral lantern. Although this version is crafted from a purchased hanging candle jar, you can easily craft your own from scratch using a widemouthed Mason jar and heavy silver wire. Use these romantic candle lanterns to decorate tabletops, line a walkway, or hang them from tree branches to light up the night.

Materials List

- glass hanging candle jar, 5" (13cm) high with a 3 1/4" (8cm) opening
- an assortment of artificial leaves and flowers (with stems removed)
- glass votive candleholder, 3" (8cm) high with a 2" (5cm) diameter opening
- votive candle
- Delta Ceramcoat Crystal Candle Gel, 10 oz. package
- 5/16" (8mm) sheer pink ribbon
- two 1/2" (1cm) miniature self-adhesive pink paper roses
- eleven round acrylic jewels (four pink, four yellow and three crystal)
- pink rose petals to sprinkle around lantern (optional)
- wooden skewer
- hot glue gun and glue sticks
- scissors
- ruler

1. Insert the glass votive candleholder into the center of the hanging candle jar.
2. Use a wooden skewer to tuck the artificial leaves and flower blooms (facing out) in between the jar and the votive candleholder.
3. Referring to the manufacturer's instructions, heat the crystal candle gel until completely melted. Immediately pour the melted candle gel into the area of the jar surrounding the votive candleholder, covering the leaves and flowers. Allow the candle gel to set.
4. Using your fingers, peel away any unwanted candle gel that may have dripped onto the edge or outer surface of the jar. You can also use a glass cleaner to clean the outer surface.
5. Insert a votive candle into the candleholder.
6. Cut two 12" (30cm) lengths of the 5/16" (8mm) pink ribbon, then tie each piece into a bow around the ends of the wire hanger. Trim the ends of the bows to the desired length, then hot glue them to secure. Hot glue a miniature pink paper rose onto the center of each bow.
7. Hot glue the acrylic jewels around the top edge of the jar.
8. For a romantic touch, sprinkle pink rose petals around the candle jar.

Floral Heart *Cake Topper*

Your wedding cake will be heavenly when crowned with this romantic floral heart wreath. Perched upon a painted glass pot base, this heart-warming creation symbolizes your everlasting love in true elegance and style. And best of all, unlike traditional cake toppers that are packed away after the wedding, the floral heart is easily removed from its base to grace your home for years to come.

Materials List

- glass (or clay) pot, 3¼" (8cm) high x 4" (10cm) in diameter
- Delta Ceramcoat Light Ivory acrylic paint
- Delta Ceramcoat matte interior varnish
- 6" (15cm) extruded foam heart
- 3" (8cm) foam ball
- green sheet moss
- floral candle ring to fit around bottom of pot, 6" (15cm) wide with a 2½" (6cm) diameter center opening
- artificial floral trims (with stems removed): nine 1½" (4cm) pink paper roses; twenty ¾" (2cm) miniature pink and cream paper roses; seven ½" (1cm) miniature self-adhesive pink paper roses; and clusters of cream baby's breath
- 9mm pearl string
- ⅞" (2cm) sheer pink wired ribbon
- iridescent crystal and ultra-fine glitter
- ½" (1cm) ivory braided trim
- if using glass pot: rubbing alcohol (70%) or Delta Ceramdecor Air-Dry PermEnamel Surface Conditioner (optional)
- floral spray adhesive (optional)
- small piece of sponge
- two 2½" (6cm) floral picks
- sharp knife
- hot glue gun and glue sticks
- scissors
- ruler

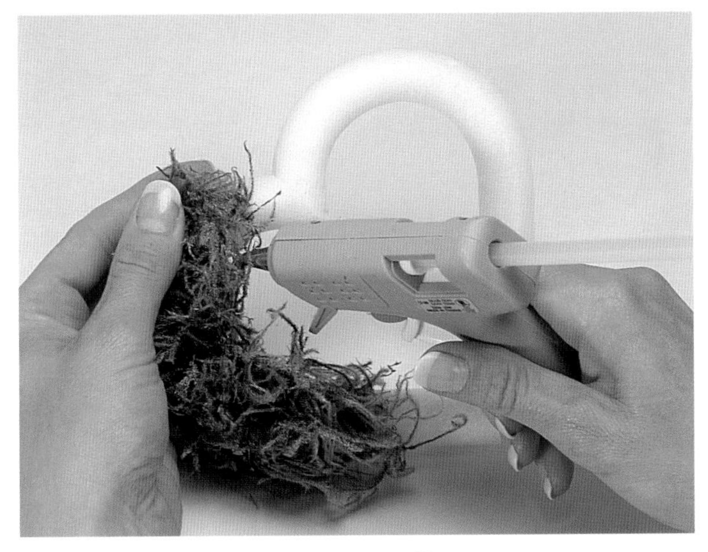

1 *Adhere Sheet Moss to Foam Heart*
Hot glue the green sheet moss around the foam heart, covering it completely. Apply the hot glue generously to the surface of the heart in small sections, pressing the moss into the glue to secure it. If you like, you could also use a floral spray adhesive to adhere the moss to the heart.

2 *Wrap Pearl String around Heart*
Wrap a 44" (112cm) piece of pearl string around the moss-covered heart, using hot glue to secure it.

3 *Adhere Roses to Heart*
Hot glue six of the 1 1/2" (4cm) pink paper roses spaced evenly around the moss-covered heart. Begin by gluing one rose at the top of the heart and one rose at the bottom of the heart and position two on each side using the first two roses as a spacing guide.

4 *Add Remaining Floral Trims*
Hot glue twenty 3/4" (2cm) pink and cream paper roses and the clusters of artificial baby's breath onto the moss-covered heart to fill in the areas between the larger roses.

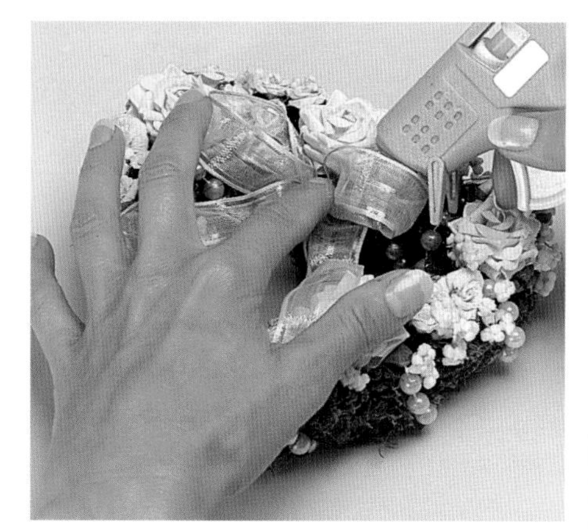

5 *Add Bow*
Tie a bow with a 22" (56cm) length of the 7/8" (2cm) pink wired ribbon, and trim the ends of the bow to the desired length. Hot glue it onto the top center of the heart.

6 *Paint Pot*
If you are using a glass pot, you can apply rubbing alcohol or a surface conditioner to the outer surface of the pot to allow the paint to adhere more quickly and easily. (If you omit this step, you'll simply apply more coats of paint to achieve solid coverage.) Use a small piece of dampened sponge to apply Light Ivory paint to the outer surface of the pot. Repeat as necessary until the surface is solidly covered. Allow the paint to dry.

Crafty Bride Tip

When painting on glass, it can be helpful to apply rubbing alcohol or a surface conditioner such as Delta Ceramdecor Air-Dry PermEnamel before applying the paint. Surface conditioners help paint to adhere more quickly and easily to a slick glass surface. If you use the conditioner, make sure to let it dry before applying the paint. If you're not using a surface conditioner, plan to apply several coats of paint to achieve solid coverage.

7 *Add Glitter and Trims to Pot*
Apply the matte varnish to the pot. While the varnish is still wet, sprinkle the pot with iridescent crystal and ultra-fine glitter. Allow the varnish to dry. Hot glue a 13" (33cm) piece of ivory braided trim around the rim of the painted pot. Hot glue seven miniature self-adhesive paper roses on top of the braided trim, spacing them evenly around the rim.

8 *Cover Foam Base with Moss*
Use a sharp knife to cut the 3" (8cm) foam ball in half. (You'll only use one half of the ball in this project.) Hot glue green sheet moss around the top curved side of the foam base, completely covering the curved surface.

9 *Adhere Moss-Covered Base to Pot*
Hot glue the mossy foam base onto the bottom of the decorated pot. (Now the bottom of the pot actually becomes the top because the pot will be sitting upside down for the finished project.)

10 *Adhere Candle Ring to Pot*
Position the flowers on the floral candle ring as desired. Hot glue the floral candle ring to the pot by applying a generous amount of hot glue to the underside of the candle ring and pressing it firmly onto the moss-covered base.

11 *Add Trims to Candle Ring*
Hot glue the three remaining 1½" (4cm) pink paper roses spaced evenly around the candle ring. For the finishing touch, drape a 27" (69cm) piece of pearl string around the candle ring, using hot glue to secure it.

12 *Attach Floral Heart to Base of Pot*
Insert two floral picks halfway into the bottom of the heart. Apply hot glue to the ends of the floral picks, then insert them into the moss-covered foam base.

Twinkling *Lights*

There's nothing more romantic at a wedding celebration than the soft glow of twinkling white lights. For a heartwarming touch, wrap a strand of miniature white lights around a floral swag, then accent the twinkling garland with individually-crafted foam hearts. It's the perfect way to light up a bridal archway or reception table in true storybook style.

Materials List

- 6' (183cm) green leaf garland with white roses (or make your own rose garland by attaching white roses onto a leaf garland with floral wire)
- strand of twenty miniature white lights
- sheets of white craft foam
- 1/4" (6mm) white and silver-beaded craft trim
- 3" (8cm) heart-shaped cookie cutter (or use template on page 77)
- Tulip Pearl Snow White dimensional paint
- Delta Ceramcoat matte interior brush-on varnish
- iridescent crystal glitter
- thirty round acrylic crystal jewels
- floral tape
- craft utility knife or X-acto knife
- foam brush or flat paintbrush
- hot glue gun and glue sticks
- pencil
- scissors
- ler

1. Entwine the string of miniature white lights around the length of the rose garland. Secure the lights with floral tape.
2. Cut approximately 78" (198cm) of the white and silver beaded craft trim. Entwine the trim around the length of the garland, then secure with hot glue.
3. Cut out ten heart shapes from the white craft foam using a heart-shaped cookie cutter or the pattern on page 77 as a template.
4. Apply the white dimensional paint around the edge of each foam heart shape. Allow to dry.
5. Using a craft knife, cut a small slit in the center of each foam heart shape. The slit should be large enough to insert a miniature white light.
6. Apply the matte varnish onto the heart shapes. While the varnish is still wet, sprinkle the surface with the iridescent crystal glitter. Allow to dry.
7. Hot glue three crystal acrylic jewels onto each heart, with two spaced evenly at the top and the third one at the bottom.
8. Insert the first light on the garland into the center slit of one of the foam hearts. Continue to attach the remaining hearts onto every second light on the garland.

Fairytale

Add a romantic ambience to your wedding reception with these handcrafted toasting flutes. Embellished with an assortment of artificial floral trims, they're the perfect way to toast a fairytale dream come true. For a charming variation, pour water into each glass and place a miniature floating candle in each one to light up the night with pure storybook enchantment.

❤ Materials List ❤

- glass champagne flutes
- Delta Ceramcoat matte interior brush-on varnish
- iridescent crystal and ultra-fine glitter
- three large artificial green leaves for each glass, approximately 4½" (11cm)
- green sheet moss
- artificial green berry sprigs
- assortment of artificial flowers (with stems removed)
- foam brush or flat paintbrush
- hot glue gun and glue sticks

1. Apply the matte varnish onto the front of the leaves. While the varnish is still wet, sprinkle the leaves with the iridescent crystal and ultra-fine glitter. The glittered leaves will look as though they've been sprinkled with magic fairy dust. Allow to dry.
2. Hot glue the glittered leaves, overlapping one another, around the top of the stem of the champagne flute. The glittered sides of the leaves should be facing outwards.
3. Hot glue the green sheet moss around the bottom of the leaves.
4. Hot glue the clusters of artificial green berries to accent the leaves.
5. For the final touch, hot glue the artificial flowers onto the glass flutes.
6. If you are using your toasting flutes as candleholders, simply fill each glass with water, add a small floating candle and light it.

Tasty Treat *Table Numbers*

Give your guests a sweet surprise with these Tasty Treat Table Numbers. Simply wrap jumbo chocolate bars with scrapbook paper, then accent them with wooden numbers and a variety of romantic trims. Add a coordinating place card with a printed message that instructs your guests to sample their tasty treat once they've found their special seat!

Once you've found your
special seat, open up
this tasty treat!

Materials List

- jumbo chocolate bars, 7 1/2" x 4" (19cm x 10cm)
- scrapbook paper
  K&Company's Daisy print
- 1/4" (6mm) ivory and gold-beaded craft trim (two pieces of each for each bar)
- wooden numbers, approximately 4" (10cm) high
- Delta Ceramcoat Light Ivory acrylic paint
- Delta Ceramcoat matte interior brush-on varnish
- ultra-fine glitter
- 5/16" (8mm) sheer yellow ribbon
- 2 1/4" (6cm) artificial green leaves (two for each bar)
- 3/4" (2cm) artificial cream roses (three for each bar)
- clusters of baby's breath
- decorated place cards (optional)
- paintbrushes and general painting supplies
- transparent tape
- decorative-edge scissors
- hot glue gun and glue sticks
- scissors
- ruler

1. Remove the outside wrapper from the chocolate bar, leaving the protective foil lining. Secure the back of the foil lining with a piece of transparent tape.

2. Cut the scrapbook paper into a 7" x 10 1/2" (18cm x 27cm) piece. Use decorative-edge scissors to trim the edges of the two 10 1/2" (27cm) sides. Hot glue the paper around the chocolate bar so that the glued edges are facing the back.

3. Cut two 10" (25cm) pieces of the ivory and gold-beaded craft trim. Hot glue the trim along the top and bottom of the chocolate bar. Once again, be sure that the glued edges are facing the back.

4. Basecoat the wooden numbers with Light Ivory.

5. Apply the matte varnish to the numbers. While the varnish is still wet, sprinkle them with the ultra-fine glitter.

6. Hot glue the painted numbers onto the center of the chocolate bars and the artificial floral trims onto the top. For a magical touch, you can apply matte varnish onto the leaves and sprinkle them with glitter before adhering them.

7. Tie a 12" (30cm) length of the 5/16" (8mm) yellow ribbon into a bow. Trim the ends of the bow to the desired length. Hot glue the bow to accent the floral trims.

8. For a humorous touch, add a decorative place card printed as follows: "Once you've found your special seat, open up this tasty treat!" Embellish the card with coordinating scrapbook paper and stickers.

Jeweled *Table Numbers*

Store-bought picture frames lined with scrapbook paper provide a colorful backdrop for your table numbers. Although a vintage-style frame is featured in this project, you may use your own unique wedding theme as inspiration for the type of frame you choose. After the wedding, insert a favorite photo into each frame for the perfect keepsake or gift idea.

Materials List

- picture frames with 4" x 6" (10cm x 15cm) openings (or large enough to accommodate the size of your numbers)
- wooden numbers, approximately 4" (10cm) high
- Delta Ceramcoat Ivory and Hydrangea Pink acrylic paints
- Delta Ceramcoat matte interior brush-on varnish
- ultra-fine glitter
- scrapbook paper
- round acrylic jewels: six pink and six crystal for each frame
- pieces of 3mm ivory pearl string (lengths will vary depending on the size of your wooden numbers)
- old toothbrush (for spattering)
- paintbrushes and general painting supplies
- double-sided tape
- hot glue gun and glue sticks
- pencil
- scissors
- ruler

1. Remove the backing and protective glass from the frame. Do not discard the glass as you can use the frame for its intended purpose after the wedding.
2. Trace around the backing of the frame onto a piece of scrapbook paper. Cut out the rectangular paper shape, then use double-sided tape to adhere the piece of scrapbook paper onto the backing of the frame. Insert it back into the frame.
3. Basecoat the wooden numbers with Ivory. Dip a dry paintbrush into Hydrangea Pink and wipe the excess paint off of the brush with a paper towel so that only a bit of paint remains. Brush the pink paint onto the numbers to give them a hint of color. Use an old toothbrush to spatter the numbers with the Ivory paint. Allow them to dry.
4. Apply the matte varnish to the numbers. While the varnish is still wet, sprinkle them with the ultra-fine glitter. Allow them to dry.
5. Hot glue the numbers onto the center of the scrapbook paper inside the frames. Cut pieces of the ivory pearl string to accent each number. Hot glue the pearl strings on the numbers to secure them.
6. Hot glue the acrylic jewels around the edge of the frame as desired. Note: If your table numbers are in the double digits, glue the jewels along the top and bottom only to allow enough room for both numbers.

Love Nest *Birdhouse*

With some heavenly hearts, dreamy doves, jeweled flower accents and pearl beaded trims, you can transform an ordinary wooden birdhouse into a "love nest." In keeping with the birdhouse theme, create coordinating wedding favors by decorating small drawstring sachet bags with the same paper embellishments and filling them with delectable almond "eggs." For complete instructions on making the favor bags, refer to the Scrappy Sweets Favors (page 41).

Materials List

- wooden birdhouse, approximately 9" (23cm) high with a 4" x 4½" (10cm x 11cm) base
- Delta Ceramcoat Light Ivory and Dusty Plum acrylic paints
- Delta Ceramcoat matte interior spray varnish
- 4mm white pearl string
- 2.5mm white pearl string
- an assortment of wedding-themed three-dimensional scrapbook embellishments
  LIKE JOLEE'S BOUTIQUE WHITE FLORAL HEARTS, DOVES AND LAVENDER JEWELED FLOWERS
- old toothbrush (for spattering)
- paintbrushes and general painting supplies
- hot glue gun and glue sticks
- scissors
- ruler

1. Basecoat the birdhouse with Light Ivory. Paint the base and the rooftop with Dusty Plum.

2. Using an old toothbrush, spatter the entire birdhouse with Light Ivory.

3. Apply the matte spray varnish.

4. Cut and glue pieces of the 4mm white pearl string to fit the two front edges and the four edges of the rooftop. (Be sure to measure first.)

5. Cut two 3" (8cm) pieces of the 2.5mm white pearl string. Glue the ends of each piece to form a loop, then hot glue the two pearl loops onto the top center of the rooftop.

6. Hot glue the heart trim onto the center of the pearl loops. Glue a miniature lavender flower trim onto the top center of the heart.

7. Hot glue the remaining scrapbook trims as desired to decorate the birdhouse. You may also add a ribbon printed with the words "Happy Wedding." If desired, you can make a placecard decorated with scrapbook embellishments to accent your love nest, as pictured above.

When We Were Young *Candy Bouquet*

Add a fun and festive touch to your wedding-day celebrations with this colorful candy bouquet centerpiece. The fun starts when you choose two of your favorite childhood photos to accent the clay-pot base. Floral foam glued inside the pot allows you to insert a medley of tasty treats and party favors. For the finishing touch, add a bouquet of foam flowers, mini drink umbrellas and a jumbo pinwheel in the center. This sweet arrangement is sure to be a hit with kids of all ages!

❤ Materials List ❤

- clay pot, 5" (13cm)
- Delta Ceramcoat satin découpage medium
- colorful tissue paper
- color-copied childhood photos of bride and groom, approximately 2 1/4" x 3" (6cm x 8cm)
- floral foam brick
- wooden dowels, 1/8" x 12" (3mm x 30cm)
- colorful paper shredding or excelsior
- five foam flowers with circle centers (or make your own flowers using sheets of craft foam and the templates on page 77)
- assortment of wrapped candies, lollipops, candy necklaces and bracelets
- three party blowers
- jumbo pinwheel
- party drink umbrellas
- alphabet beads to spell name of bride and groom
- colorful curling ribbon
- sharp knife
- foam brush or flat paintbrush
- hot glue gun and glue sticks
- scissors

1. Tear the tissue paper into small pieces, then apply the pieces to the clay pot using the découpage medium. Apply additional coats of découpage medium over the surface of the tissue paper to seal it. Allow to dry in between coats.

2. Use your fingers to tear around the main image of the color-copied photos to create a textured edge. Use the découpage medium to adhere the two photos onto the front of the pot. Apply several coats of the découpage medium to seal the surface of the photos. Allow to dry in between coats. Hot glue alphabet beads beside the photos to spell the names of the bride and groom.

3. Using a sharp knife, cut the floral foam brick to fit inside the clay pot. Hot glue it to the inside of the pot to secure it.

4. Insert the jumbo pinwheel into the center of the foam base. Then insert the three party blowers, one in the center and the remaining two on each side.

5. Hot glue the foam flowers and their circular centers onto the top of the wooden dowels. Hot glue the wrapped candies onto the stems of the wooden dowels, allowing enough space at the bottom of the dowel stems to insert them into the foam base.

6. Insert the candy-trimmed foam flowers and lollipops into the floral foam base. Then hot glue pieces of paper shredding around the trims to conceal the base.

7. Drape the candy necklaces and bracelets around the foam flowers and lollipops. Hot glue individually-wrapped candies as desired to accent the base of the centerpiece.

8. For a festive touch, add colorful drink umbrellas and curling ribbon.

NEUTRO
HEALTHY

Happily Ever After

It's time for you to celebrate the most important chapter of your wedding story—sharing a lifetime of joy and happiness. You've crafted the wedding of your dreams, and like most newlyweds, you'll be anxiously waiting for those all-important wedding photos to arrive. In this chapter you'll find picture-perfect ideas for showcasing your treasured wedding memories and also for transforming wedding photos into one-of-a-kind gifts and keepsakes.

Memory albums are a must for every bride, and the unique collage design featured in this section (page 68) introduces you to a simple découpage technique using floral napkins, delicate doilies and a variety of scrapbook papers and trims. Using this same découpage technique, you can transform an ordinary paint bucket into a sentimental time capsule (page 76) perfect for storing your wedding and honeymoon mementos.

You'll also discover how to make a gorgeous video case (page 74) and Vintage Picture Frame (page 71) to showcase your favorite wedding photos with elegance and style. And in just a few easy steps, you can craft the Wedding Keepsake Candle (page 72) to add a soft, romantic glow to your home décor.

Your wedding photos will no doubt be your most treasured wedding keepsake. So don't keep them stored away. Let your photos inspire you to showcase, share and cherish your wedding memories with love and happiness as you celebrate your future together. Happy ever after!

Collage
Memory Album

Using a simple découpage technique, a blank memory book becomes an enchanting keepsake when adorned with a favorite wedding photo and an assortment of floral napkins and scrapbook trims. Fine-crochet doilies provide an interesting background texture, while the vintage-style buttons, pearl beading and romantic ribbon bow add the perfect finishing touch.

Materials List

- ivory memory book, 9" x 11" (23cm x 28cm)
- Delta Ceramcoat satin découpage medium
- floral wedding napkins
  BRIDAL RIBBONS BY PARTY EXPRESS
- scrapbook papers in pale green and cream
  ANNA GRIFFIN SAGE GREEN TONE AND AMSCAN WHITE ROSES
- color-copied wedding photo, preferably 5" x 7" (13cm x 18cm)
- two 6" (15cm) white (or ivory) round fine-crochet doilies
- floral stickers
  K&COMPANY'S WHITE FLOWERS EMBOSSED STICKERS
- white wedding-themed, three-dimensional scrapbook trims
  JOLEE'S BOUTIQUE WHITE FLORAL HEARTS AND DOVES
- three 1/2" (1cm) ivory vintage-style buttons
- three 1/2" (1cm) miniature self-adhesive white or ivory paper roses
- 3mm ivory pearl string
- 1/4" (6mm) ivory ribbon
- foam brush or flat paintbrush
- hot glue gun and glue sticks
- scissors
- ruler

Dream Idea
Magical Memories Photo Album

It's easy to transform a store-bought photo album into a one-of-a-kind personalized keepsake. Just purchase a pre-cut photo mat to showcase your favorite wedding photo. Hot glue the mat with the photo onto the cover of your album, then embellish the mat with an assortment of artificial flowers, romantic ribbons and crafty trims.

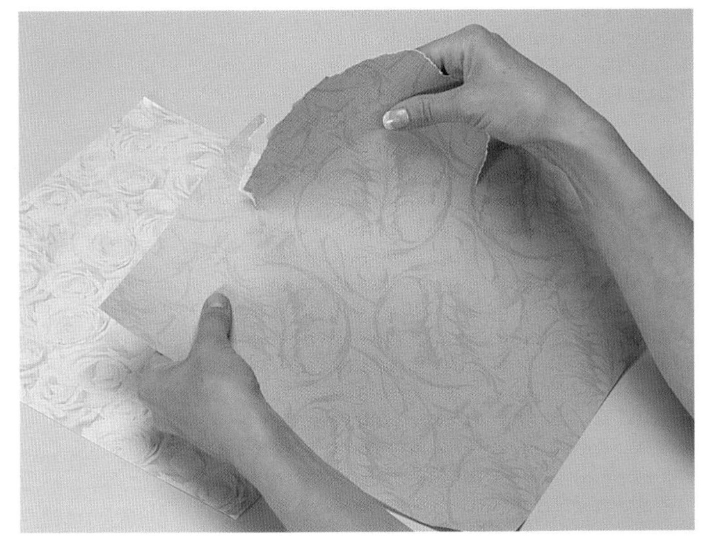

1 *Tear Pieces of Scrapbook Paper*

Tear out two pieces (approximately 6" [15cm] in diameter) of decorative paper, one from the pale green scrapbook paper and one from the cream scrapbook paper. The torn edges will give the album a textured, handcrafted look.

2 *Découpage Paper onto Album*

Using the découpage medium, adhere the torn piece of cream scrapbook paper onto the upper left corner of the album and the torn piece of pale green paper onto the bottom right corner. When adhering the paper, simply use a large flat brush or a foam brush to paint the découpage medium onto the backs of the torn pieces. Then apply additional coats of découpage medium over the top of the torn pieces to seal the surface of the paper. Allow the paper to dry in between coats.

3 *Découpage Napkins onto Album*

Tear three pieces from the floral napkins (approximately 4" [10cm] in diameter) and use the découpage medium to adhere each piece onto the album, with two pieces overlapping at the top and the third piece on the lower left side. Apply additional coats of découpage medium over the surface of the napkins to seal them. Allow the surface to dry in between coats.

4 *Découpage Doilies onto Album*

Saturate the two fine-crochet doilies with the découpage medium by applying the medium liberally to one side of each doily with a foam brush (the découpage medium will soak through the entire doily) and adhere them to the album, overlapping them in the center. Apply additional coats of the découpage medium over the doilies. Allow them to dry in between coats.

5 *Découpage Photo onto Album*

To give the wedding photo a textured look, use your fingers to tear around the edges of the main image to form an oval shape. Use the découpage medium to apply the photo onto the center of the memory album. Apply additional coats to seal the surface of the photo. Allow it to dry between coats.

6 *Apply Floral Stickers*

Apply floral stickers to the memory album as desired. Add visual interest by overlapping the stickers onto the edges of the wedding photo. Seal the surface of the stickers with additional coats of découpage medium. Allow the album to dry completely.

7 *Add Pearl Accents*

Form two loops with the 3 1/2" (9cm) lengths of pearl string. Hot glue both pearl loops onto the bottom center of the photo.

8 *Add Bow and Paper Rose*

Tie a bow with a 10" (25cm) length of the 1/4" (6mm) ivory ribbon and trim the ends to the desired length. Hot glue the bow onto the bottom of the pearl loops, and hot glue a miniature paper rose onto the center of the bow.

9 *Add Final Trims*

To finish, hot glue the three-dimensional scrapbook hearts onto the top left and bottom right of the photo. Glue a miniature paper rose onto the top of each heart. Glue the paper dove scrapbook trims onto the bottom left corner and the three ivory buttons onto the top right.

Vintage *Picture Frame*

Using a crackle painting technique, you can transform an inexpensive wooden frame into a vintage-style wedding keepsake. Reminiscent of a bygone era, this elegant frame is perfect for displaying a classic black-and-white or sepia-tone photograph. For a touch of romantic elegance, embellish the frame with artificial roses, acrylic jewels, pearl flowers and ribbon trims.

Materials List

- 5" x 7" (13cm x 18cm) wooden frame (outside dimensions of the frame are 7" x 9" [18cm x 23cm])
- Delta Ceramcoat Burnt Umber and Ivory acrylic paints
- Delta Ceramcoat crackle medium
- Delta Ceramcoat matte interior spray and brush-on varnish
- iridescent crystal glitter
- 1/4" (6mm) ivory and gold-beaded craft trim
- 1/4" (6mm) ivory ribbon
- four 3/4" (2cm) pearl flower trims (with stems removed)
- nine round acrylic crystal jewels
- three 1 1/2" (4cm) artificial cream roses with leaves (with stems removed)
- old toothbrush (for spattering)
- paintbrushes and general painting supplies
- hot glue gun and glue sticks
- scissors
- ruler

1. Remove the cardboard backing and protective glass from the frame.

2. Basecoat the frame with Burnt Umber. Allow it to dry. Following the manufacturer's instructions, apply an even coat of the crackle medium onto the frame. Let the crackle medium air-dry until it's tacky, then apply a light, even top coat of the Ivory paint. Allow the frame to dry. The aged, crackle effect will appear within minutes.

3. Using an old toothbrush, spatter the frame with Burnt Umber paint.

4. Apply the matte spray varnish onto the frame.

5. Cut a piece of the ivory and gold-beaded trim to measure around the opening of the frame. I use a 25 1/2" (65cm) piece, but this measurement may vary somewhat from frame to frame. Beginning at the bottom center of the frame, hot glue the trim around the opening. (By starting at the bottom center, the glued ends of the trim will be cleverly concealed by the artificial floral trims.)

6. Hot glue the four pearl flower trims onto the frame, placing one in each corner. Glue the nine crystal jewels onto the frame, spacing three evenly along the top and along each side.

7. Apply the matte brush-on varnish onto the leaves of the roses. While the varnish is still wet, sprinkle the leaves with the iridescent crystal glitter. Allow them to dry. Hot glue the three roses with the glittered leaves onto the bottom center of the frame.

8. Tie a bow using a 10" (25cm) length of the 1/4" (6mm) ivory ribbon. Trim the ends of the bow to the desired length. Hot glue the bow onto the right side of the floral trims.

9. Insert the protective glass piece back into the frame. Add your photo and secure it with the cardboard backing.

Wedding Keepsake *Candle*

Using rub-on decals, it's easier than you think to create the hand-painted look of this exquisite keepsake candle. Once you've applied your floral background motif, you simply découpage a favorite wedding photo onto the candle, and then accent it with a wreath of artificial blooms and romantic ribbon trims. Light the candle on your first anniversary to relive the magical memories of your special day. Or you can use your engagement photo to create an elegant unity candle to light during your wedding ceremony.

Materials List

- ivory pillar candle, 8" (20cm) high and 3" (8cm) in diameter
- color-copied wedding photo with main image of about 3" (8cm) in diameter
- 3 1/2" (9cm) circle template (see page 77)
- flower decals
  PLAID FOLKART ONE STROKE DECALS: WISTERIA & DAISIES
- Delta Ceramcoat satin découpage medium
- iridescent crystal glitter
- lavender and yellow artificial floral trims (with stems removed): 3/4" (2cm) miniature lavender roses with leaves, 3/4" (2cm) miniature yellow paper roses, tiny clusters of silk lavender flowers with berries, and 3/4" (2cm) miniature white and yellow daisies
- 12" (30cm) of 5/16" (8mm) sheer lavender ribbon
- 1 1/4" (3cm) lavender beaded pearl flower trim
- small piece of sponge
- foam brush or flat paintbrush
- hot glue gun and glue sticks
- scissors
- ruler

Crafty Bride Tip

A simple trick for drawing a perfect circle around your photo image is to use a glass with a 3 1/2" (9cm) diameter opening to trace around. You'll be able to see the image through the glass so that you'll know for sure that everything fits.

You can also refer to the circle pattern on page 77 or use a circular drawing compass to trace the circle shape onto a piece of lightweight cardboard. After the circle shape is cut out, it can be used as a template to trace around the image of your photo.

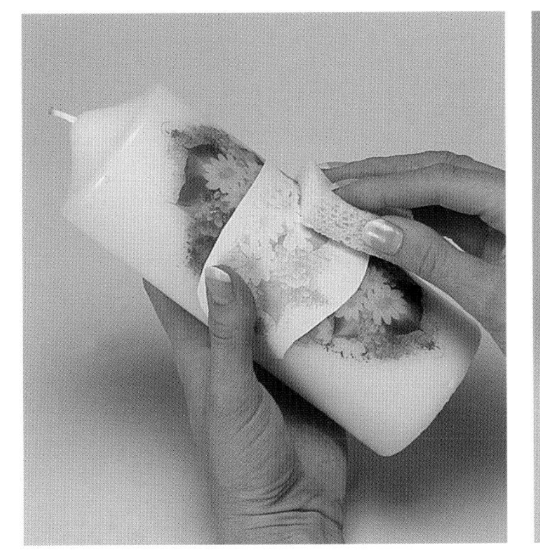

1 *Apply Decals*

Referring to the manufacturer's instructions, use a dampened piece of sponge to apply the floral decals to the candle in a pleasing arrangement. (I use three of the medium-size decals, with the two matching ones at the top and bottom and the third slightly longer one placed horizontally in the center.) Allow the decals to dry. Apply several coats of the découpage medium to seal the surface of the floral decals. Allow the medium to dry between coats.

2 *Cut Out Photo*

Trace around the photo image using a 3$^{1}/_{2}$" (9cm) circle template (see Crafty Bride Tip, page 72). Cut out the circular shape with scissors.

3 *Découpage Photo onto Candle*

Apply a generous amount of découpage medium onto the back of the circular photo and press it firmly onto the center of the floral decals on the candle until it is secure. Smooth the photo to remove any unwanted creases and allow it to set. Then apply several more coats of découpage medium to seal the surface of the photo. Allow the medium to dry in between coats.

4 *Glue Floral Trims Around Circular Photo*

Apply an additional coat of découpage medium to the floral decals around the outside edges of the photo. While the medium is still wet, sprinkle the decals with iridescent crystal glitter. Allow it to dry. Hot glue the floral trims around the wedding photo, alternating between the lavender and yellow roses, the clusters of flowers with berries and the white and yellow daisies. Arrange the flowers as you like, creating a pleasing composition.

5 *Add Final Trims*

Tie a 12" (30cm) length of the $^{5}/_{16}$" (8mm) lavender ribbon in a bow and trim the ends to the desired length. Hot glue the bow just beneath the bottom of the floral trims. To finish, hot glue the beaded flower trim onto the center of the bow. If desired, set the candle on a round or square glass candleholder sprinkled with potpourri and artificial daisy blooms.

Wedding *Video Case*

It's easy to transform an ordinary plastic video case into an extraordinary wedding keepsake! To make this lovely video case cover, a piece of fleece backing is sewn onto heavy brocade fabric, then accented with lace and pearl-beaded trim. Once the fabric cover is glued onto the outside of the video case, it is embellished with a romantic wedding photo and an assortment of white satin roses, bows and pearl sprays.

Materials List

- white plastic video case, 5 1/2" x 9" (14cm x 23cm)
- piece of heavy white brocade fabric, 8 1/2" x 11 3/4" (22cm x 30cm)
- piece of white fleece, 8 1/2" x 11 3/4" (22cm x 30cm)
- white thread
- 1 1/4" (3cm) white lace trim
- 4mm white pearl string,
- 1/2" (1cm) white braided trim to trim photo sleeve
- 1/8" (3mm) white ribbon
- three 1/2" (1cm) miniature white satin roses
- 3mm white pearl spray
- self-adhesive photo mounting sleeve to fit a 4" x 6" (10cm x 15cm) photo
- 4" x 6" (10cm x 15cm) wedding photo
- sewing machine
- hot glue gun and glue sticks
- scissors
- ruler

Crafty Bride Tip

The measurements listed in the materials and instructions are based on a 5 1/2" x 9" (14cm x 23cm) standard-size video case. However, since video cases can vary somewhat in size, you may have to adjust your measurements accordingly. If you are using a different size video case, simply open up the case and measure the total dimensions before beginning the project. Remember that it's always best to confirm your measurements before cutting any of the materials.

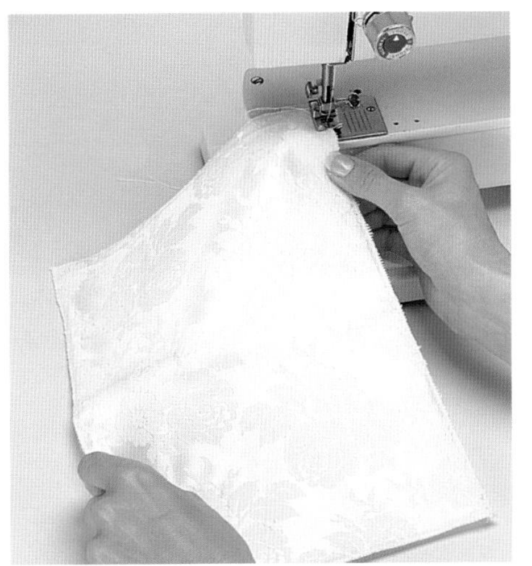

1 *Sew Fleece onto Fabric*
Measure the video case and cut out one piece each of the fleece and the brocade fabric to cover the outer surface of the video case, including the spine. Stitch the fleece backing onto the back side of the fabric with a sewing machine and white thread by zig-zagging the raw edges together.

2 *Add Lace Trim*
Measure the lace trim to fit around the entire edge of the fleece-backed fabric piece, approximately 40" to 42" (102cm to 107cm) for a standard-size case. Use the sewing machine to sew the lace trim around the edge of the fabric and trim away any excess.

3 *Adhere Fabric to Video Case*
Hot glue the lace-trimmed fabric piece onto the outer surface of the video case.

4 *Add Pearl Trim and Photo Sleeve*
Cut a piece of the 4mm pearl string to fit around the case, approximately 40" to 42" (102cm to 107cm). Hot glue the pearl string around the edge of the lace. Trim a bit off the length of the photo sleeve and photo, approximately 3/4" (2cm), so that its size is proportionate to the video case. Hot glue the photo mounting sleeve onto the front center of the video case. Hot glue four pieces of braided trim around the edge of the photo sleeve, with the two 4 1/2" (11cm) pieces at the top and bottom and the two 5 3/4" (15cm) pieces on each side (be careful not to glue the top opening shut). Cut approximately 21" (53cm) of the pearl string and hot glue it around the center of the braided trim. Begin gluing the pearls from the bottom center of the trim so that the glued edges will be concealed by the satin roses.

5 *Add Final Trims*
Find the center of a 57" (145cm) length of 1/8" (3mm) white ribbon and form four loops of equal length on each side of the center by looping the ribbon back and forth. Secure the loops in the center with a 6 1/2" (17cm) piece of 1/8" (3mm) white ribbon. Hot glue the bow onto the bottom center of the braided trim. Hot glue the pearl spray and the three white satin roses onto the center of the bow. To finish, insert a favorite wedding photo into the photo sleeve.

Wedding Memories
Time Capsule

Using a quick and easy découpage technique, you can transform a newly purchased paint can into a beautiful time capsule for storing your cherished wedding and honeymoon mementos. It's perfect for storing those bulky items that are difficult to preserve in a flat memory album. For a romantic touch, open your time capsule on each anniversary to relive those once-in-a-lifetime wedding and honeymoon memories for years to come.

Materials List

- newly purchased one gallon paint can
- Delta Ceramcoat acrylic paint in Light Ivory, Wedgwood Green and Metallic Silver
- Delta Ceramcoat satin découpage medium
- iridescent crystal and ultra-fine glitter
- floral napkins
  HYDRANGEA BRANCH BY KELLER-CHARLES
- color-copied wedding photo (torn image is approximately 5" [13cm] wide)
- three-dimensional scrapbook stickers and photo corners
  K&COMPANY'S POPPY POP-UPS
- artificial floral trims in dusty blue, pale green and cream (with stems removed): roses, hydrangea blooms and sprigs of cream baby's breath
- 2½" (6cm) sheer white wired ribbon with pearl trim
- small piece of sponge
- old toothbrush (for spattering)
- paintbrushes and general painting supplies
- hot glue gun and glue sticks
- scissors
- ruler

1. Remove the lid of the can. Use a small piece of dampened sponge to paint the outer surface of the can and lid with Light Ivory. Apply several coats to achieve solid coverage. Allow it to dry in between coats.
2. Very sparingly, use the sponge to apply Metallic Silver to add a textured effect to the painted surface.
3. Using an old toothbrush, spatter the surface with Wedgwood Green. Allow paint to dry.
4. Tear the floral napkins into several pieces of various sizes. Apply the torn pieces of napkins onto the can with the découpage medium, overlapping each piece as desired. (For visual interest and contrast, leave some painted areas of the can exposed.) Apply additional coats of découpage medium over the surface of the napkins to seal them. Allow it to dry in between coats.
5. To give your wedding photo a textured look, use your fingers to tear around the edges of the main image in a rectangular shape. Use the découpage medium to apply the photo onto the front center of the can at a slight angle. Apply additional coats to seal. Allow it to dry.
6. Apply a final coat of the découpage medium onto the napkins (not the photo). While the découpage medium is still wet, sprinkle the surface of the napkins with the iridescent crystal and ultra-fine glitter. Allow it to dry.
7. Hot glue the three-dimensional photo corners and scrapbook stickers as desired to embellish the wedding photo.
8. Hot glue the floral trims onto the lid, then place it back onto the can.
9. Tie a bow using a 42" (107cm) length of the 2½" (6cm) ribbon. Hot glue the bow onto the lid of the can, to the left side of the floral trims. Entwine the ends of the ribbon around the handle as desired.

Patterns

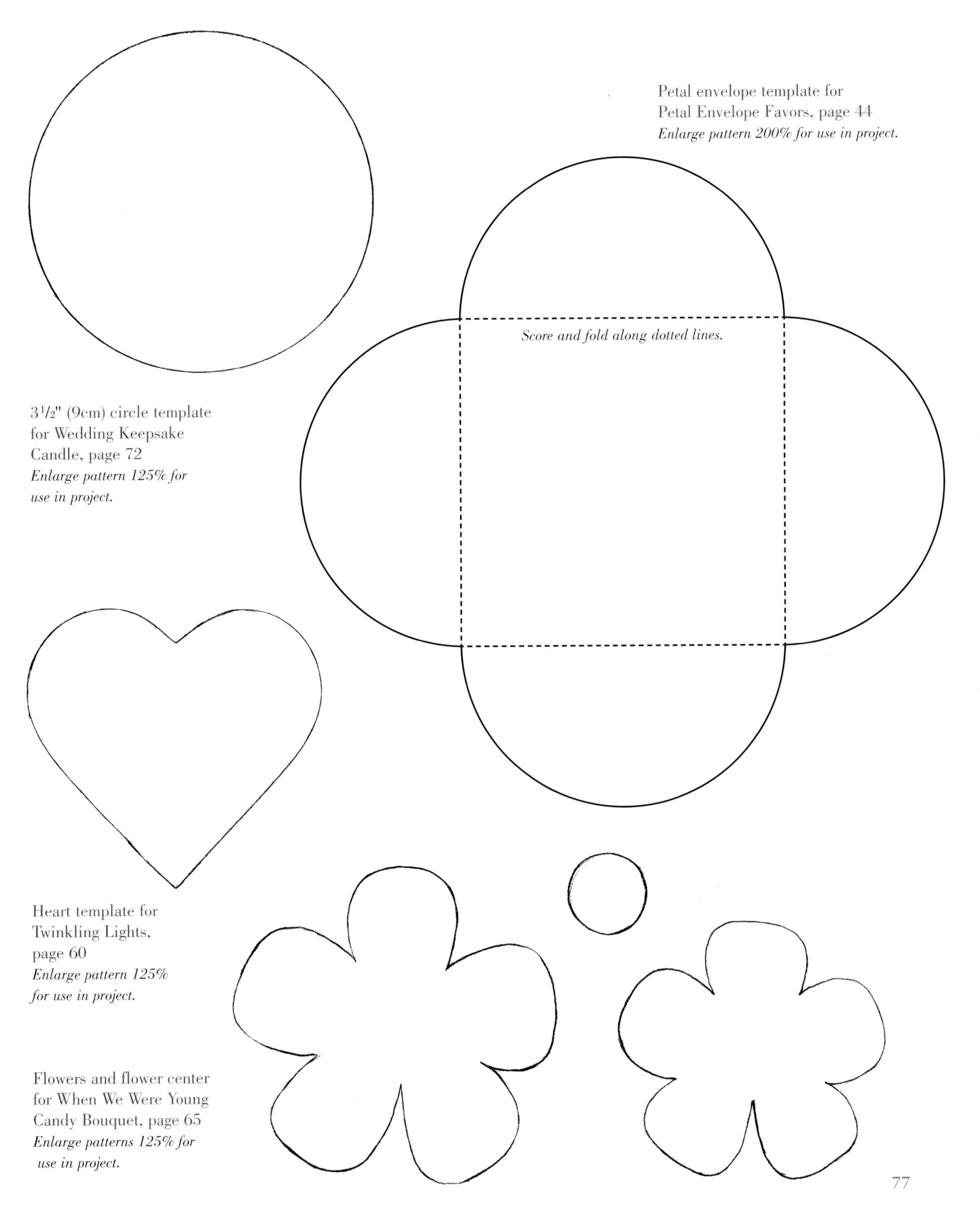

Petal envelope template for
Petal Envelope Favors, page 44
Enlarge pattern 200% for use in project.

3½" (9cm) circle template
for Wedding Keepsake
Candle, page 72
*Enlarge pattern 125% for
use in project.*

Heart template for
Twinkling Lights,
page 60
*Enlarge pattern 125%
for use in project.*

Flowers and flower center
for When We Were Young
Candy Bouquet, page 65
*Enlarge patterns 125% for
use in project.*

Resources

All of the materials used to make the projects in this book can be purchased at your local craft, fabric, scrapbooking and rubber-stamping stores or at discount department stores. Be sure to check out the wedding section in your local craft store for specialty items and for lots of great ideas. If you are unable to find what you need at a local store, contact the manufacturers listed below for a retailer near you.

Anna Griffin, Inc.
733 Lambert Drive
Atlanta, GA 30324
(888) 817-8170 or
(404) 817-8170
www.annagriffin.com
❤ *Anna Griffin line of scrapbook papers*

Delta Technical Coatings, Inc.
2550 Pellissier Place
Whittier, CA 90601
(800) 423-4135
www.deltacrafts.com
❤ *Delta Ceramcoat acrylic paints, matte interior spray and brush-on varnish, satin découpage medium, crackle medium and general painting supplies*

DMD Industries, Inc.
2300 S. Old Missouri Road
Springdale, AR 72764
(800) 805-9890
(479) 750-8929
www.dmdind.com
❤ *memory books and scrapbook supplies*

EK Success
P.O. Box 1141
Clifton, NJ 07014
www.eksuccess.com
www.stickopotamus.com
❤ *Jolee's Boutique line of scrapbooking trims*

FloraCraft (Dow Styrofoam)
One Longfellow Place
P.O. Box 400
Ludington, MI 49431
(800) 253-0409
www.floracraft.com
www.styrofoamcrafts.com
❤ *Styrofoam brand plastic foam products*

Hirschberg Schutz & Co., Inc.
650 Liberty Avenue
Union, NJ 07083
(800) 543-5442
(908) 810-1111
❤ *Modern Romance line of wedding trims*

K&Company, LLC
8500 N.W. River Park Drive
Pillar #136
Parkville, MO 64152
(888) 244-2083 or
(816) 389-4150
www.kandcompany.com
❤ *scrapbook papers, stickers and embellishments*

Loew-Cornell, Inc.
563 Chestnut Avenue
Teaneck, NJ 07666
(201) 836-7070
www.loew-cornell.com
❤ *paintbrushes and general painting supplies*

Plaid Enterprises, Inc.
P.O. Box 7600
Norcross, GA 30091
(800) 842-4197
www.plaidonline.com
❤ *Plaid FolkArt One Stroke Decals*

Index

Find more
creative wedding ideas and inspiration *in other fine North Light and Memory Makers Books!*

These books and other fine titles are available from your local art & craft retailer, bookstore, online supplier or by calling 1-800-448-0915.

Wedding Papercrafts
by the Editors of North Light Books
In projects using the latest techniques in papercrafting, rubber stamping and collage, *Wedding Papercrafts* shows you how to create your own invitations, decorations and favors. All of the projects show you how to personalize your wedding with unique handmade touches. The book includes 50 gorgeous projects made easy with patterns and step-by-step instruction.
ISBN 1-55870-653-4, paperback, 128 pages, #70603-K

Scrapbooking Your Wedding
by the Editors of Memory Makers Books
Your wedding day is one of the most precious days in your life. Keep the memories close to your heart by creating a scrapbook to hold all of the beautiful pictures and mementos from the day. In *Scrapbooking Your Wedding*, you'll find hundreds of ways to create pages as beautiful as your special day. In addition, the book includes photo lists, tips for taking wedding pictures and more.

ISBN 1-892127-46-6, paperback, 128 pages, #33211-K

Simply Beautiful Greeting Cards
by Heidi Boyd
Whether you're a complete beginner or a seasoned crafter, *Simply Beautiful Greeting Cards* shows you how to create personalized greeting cards for every occasion. You'll find cards that are great for holidays, birthdays, weddings and "just because." With 50 different quick and easy cards to choose from, you'll be eager to show your family and friends how much you care with style and flair. In addition to the wide array of cards, you'll find a helpful section on basic tools and materials as well as a treasure trove of papercrafting tips and tricks.
ISBN 1-58180-564-0, paperback, 128 pages, #33019-K

Creative Wedding Showers
by Laurie Dewberry
Whether you'd like to throw a traditional hen party or a nontraditional couples shower, the ten shower themes in *Creative Wedding Showers* will give you plenty of ideas and inspiration. From recipes for the perfect party snacks and meals to games and favors, this book has everything you need to throw a wonderful shower that suits the bride-to-be.

You'll find step-by-step instructions for making invitations, decorations and even party favors that will show you how to give an unforgettable shower.
ISBN 1-55870-710-7, paperback, 96 pages, #70662-K